Filling Up the Brown Bag

Filling Up
the Brown Bag

(a children's sermon how-to book)

by
Jerry Marshall Jordan

Illustrated by Mary Lou Anderson

The Pilgrim Press
Cleveland, Ohio

The Pilgrim Press
Cleveland, Ohio 44115

© 1987 by The Pilgrim Press

Printed in the United States of America
The paper used in this publication is acid free and meets the
minimum requirements of American National Standard for
Information Sciences-Permanence of Paper for Printed Library
Materials, ANSI Z39.48-1984

97 96 95 94 93 92   10 9 8 7 6 5 4

Library of Congress Cataloging-in-Publication Data
Jordan, Jerry Marshall, 1937–
Filling up the brown bag.

1. Preaching to children.   I. Title.
BV4235.C4J67   1987   251'.0088054   87-12963
ISBN 0-8298-0759-4 (pbk.)

For the children of
First Congregational Church
United Church of Christ
Colorado Springs, Colorado

Contents

(Listed by Subject)

Filling Up the Brown Bag

Preface

This is a book without chapters. Why? Because all the topics discussed in this book are parts of the whole, and the book really should be read that way.

"What is the use of a book," thought Alice, "without pictures or conversations?"[1] This book has some pictures, though they are not of my adventures in wonderland. Rather, they help to illustrate the subject under discussion, i.e., children's sermons. As for "conversations," I am taking this opportunity to discuss with you on these pages *how* I do children's sermons. The question "Shall we have sermons for children?" has been answered affirmatively long ago. I hope this homiletical exploration helps all who have the privilege of doing children's sermons.

Children's sermons are no recent phenomenon. While looking through the historical records of the church I am serving, I was surprised to find this brief note in "The Congregational News," by the Rev. Roselle Theodore Cross: "I expect to resume the five-minute sermons for children."[2] Date: September 18, 1879!

Another example predated the Civil War. Pastor Edward Parmelee Smith gave sermons for children in Pepperell, Massachusetts, as reported in *Gerty's Papa's Civil War*, edited by William H. Armstrong (Pilgrim, 1984). Surely someone in the early church must have also proposed to do this in the worship setting. Perhaps such an effort was inspired by the biblical passage where Jesus welcomed the children. Though the Gospel writers do not say so, certainly Jesus also spoke to the children. Since

3

then, we can rightly imagine that someone, somewhere, at sometime or other in each century has spoken to the children in a way that might be called a "children's sermon" by us today. In our own century, this mode of communication has become more and more popular. In my library I have children's sermon books that date back into the '30s and '40s, as well as the '50s and '60s. However, in the '70s and '80s, the children's sermon has really become a standard part of many church services. It has truly come of age! Still the question is asked, even by those who have been presenting these youth sermons for years (and especially by those just out of seminary, or lay persons who are asked to do this), "How do you do it?" Because this question has so often been put to me, I now want to explain informally, to the best of my ability, how I do it. Accordingly, I have chosen to use the conversational style, first person, throughout the following pages.

We tend to laugh at how-to books, that is until we too need to know "how-to." Rather than just calling this book a how-to of children's sermons, I have chosen instead the process that engages me weekly, that of "filling up the brown bag." The brown bag has become my symbol, for that is what I use to conceal a prop until I am ready to show it to the children. My children's sermon books are a brown bag trilogy, using bag terminology in each title.[3]

This book is about how I fill up my brown bag, so to speak. "Filling" is an action word and that is what is required. The concern here is how I (and you, too) do children's sermons, which requires more than just finding and putting a prop into a brown bag. It is my hope that this book will be helpful in the writing and delivery of children's sermons.

I have had a lot of encouragement from parents—

4

and children—during my almost two decades of doing children's sermons. From the children come eager expressions and responsive answers, in short, their enthusiasm which each week takes me back to my task with renewed dedication. On those times when my sermon for them is subpar, I so much want to say to them, "I'm sorry!" But because children are so refreshingly receptive, I know already—in advance (from experience)—that they will welcome me back the next time around as if last week's poor sermon did not happen. For me, this is *grace*. And it makes me try all the harder!

Many thanks to the readers of my manuscript. These friends are the Rev. Dr. Robert Frykholm,[4] Sara Lynn Weatherman,[5] the Rev. Dr. Annabel Clark,[6] Dr. P. Roy Brammell,[7] and Lavonne Eliason.[8] To my wonderful artist, truly a gracious person, Mary Lou Anderson,[9] I owe a big *thank you*. Then, to the most valuable of all my advisers and helpers, Gayle,[10] I express my unending thanks—and *love*.

Filling Up the Brown Bag

Children's sermons. Where do we begin? With theology, of course! Would we think of building a house without a firm foundation? That is what theology is to good children's sermons.

Children's sermons and theology *do mix* when we begin with where the children are, with their experiences out of which arise the existential questions that require adequate theological answers. It is as Roger Shinn has stated:

> Any time a person asks a serious question and relates that question to the important purposes of his [her] life, he [she] deals with theology. When he [she] uses religious language, the question is obviously theological. If he [she] avoids the phraseology of religion, the theology is hidden in the question. In our world we hear questions of both kinds. Anyone with a sharp ear can pick up a list of theological questions in a normal week of living. Sometimes such questions are not even verbalized, but are implied in responses persons make to the happenings around them.[11]

Certainly, the community of faith (e.g., the church and the home, provided the latter is religiously inclined) impacts children's lives in more ways than we often think possible, causing them to think about God, Jesus, prayer, right and wrong, etc., which in turn prompts questions that do not just come "out of the blue." Not to begin with the children's "whys?"—however asked—is to miss a vital connecting link in communicating with our children about the great theological truths of the faith that we want them to explore, to understand, and to live.

The children we minister to come to and from life's experiences asking theological questions, even when the word theological is too big for them to pronounce or understand. Some experiences are so profound in and of themselves (e.g., birth, death, suffering, disappointment, as well as wonder, joy, hope, love) that the ultimate questions arising from them require some profound answers simply stated. This is the opportunity for theological perspective presented to us as the children sit around us on the chancel steps each Sunday.

There is yet a more basic consideration which must be pondered. *Revelation.* Here reference is to the issue of the revelatory nature of God. It is doubtful that we would get very far with children's sermons without revelation, or for that matter with sermons for adults, or with any other theological understanding we might attempt. While our children may not fully comprehend what this means, especially the younger ones, it does need to be clearly understood by us. "This is," as articulated by John Macquarrie, "the primary source of theology, and is also a basic category in theological thinking."[12] In essence, God wants to be known, to be perceived by us. Instead of remaining remote and isolated in some distant heaven, or withdrawn and hidden from us here on earth, God ever seeks to relate to us in ways that will allow the divine Mystery to be penetrated (in part, that is), thus enabling us to know life's ultimate and animating Force.

The initiative is God's! It has to be if we are to know God, for this infinite One is beyond the grasp of our finite minds. No, we have not reached this "God conclusion" through the powers of our own reason and experience, but have instead been the recipients of God's action upon our lives, giving us the gift of faith. Now, the content of this revelatory disclosure is not just divine *information*, even though that is part of what we have received. More important—and this is what really enlivens our faith-story—is that God comes to us personally. This has been supremely attested to in Jesus, the Christ. At other times, B.C. as well as A.D., and in other ways and people, God's incarnating Self has been experienced, though not with the same indwelling intensity as evidenced in Christ. As a result, God's Spirit is ever seeking to reveal the "more" of the divine Reality, which then allows us to go beyond simply knowing *about* God to a living relationship *with* God.

Much of the above is a foreign language for most of the children to whom we minister. Obviously, this is not what we talk about in our children's sermons, at least not directly, but where we are in the general overview of our theological awareness that impinges on our children as well as on us all, even when we are not consciously aware of it. It is what makes the community of faith possible, as well as being the context in which we speak with our children about God.

Surely we cannot expect our children to be miniature adults, abstracting theology as has been done in the preceding paragraphs. Neither should we expect the children's sermon to carry the whole responsibility of inspiring their response, as if it were the sole educational thrust of the church in instructing them about God's will as it relates to life, and in particular their lives. As a complement to the children's sermon, there is the ongoing curriculum work in the church school classes, not to mention the religious instruction which (we hope!) occurs in the home. Perhaps one theological truth which is communicated when the children sit on the chancel steps is the awareness that they are loved and wanted. While this is a subtle message, we who have the privilege week after week—or even for those who do it on less frequent occasions—should never overlook its import.

Is this not what Jesus communicated to those young ones who were brought to him? In Matthew's Gospel (19:13–15) we read of this happening (and we can only guess how many more times it happened as he went from town to town).

> Then children were brought to him that he might lay his hands on them and pray. The disciples rebuked the people; but Jesus said, "Let the children come to me, and do not hinder them; for to such belongs the kingdom." And he laid his hands on them and went away.

When interpreted, with our children in mind, this means that they are important to God, and they are loved by God. The church's ministry is to nurture continually this awareness of God. If we do not assist in doing this with the children's sermon, then it fails the validity test. One way we do this is talking about Jesus, what he taught and did, so that God might be known more fully. Granted, that is a big order, and thank God all of it does not have to be done in one children's sermon.

Also, within the corporate worship setting, there is a subtle benefit. Being with others at this special time and place, hearing (in their own terminology, of course), "if God so loved us, we also ought to love one another [1 John 4:11]," means taking them beyond just talking and thinking about the *Who, What,* and *Where* of God. Those we are to love are all around us. Solitary religion is not the truth being conveyed in this context. Rather, the empha-

9

sis by association and by the reference made is that we are to reach out and love in ways that make a difference in the lives of those near, kin and friend alike, as well as loving those who are difficult to love. John Westerhoff notes in his book *Values for Tomorrow's Children* that "Paul Tillich described the church's educational task as introducing each new generation into the life and mission of the faith community."[13] Well! Is that not the way to show Christian love? Here the children's sermon can have its say, making a valuable contribution in helping to inspire our children. It is also one part of the rationale (theologically speaking) of why we take the time to talk with our children in this special way. With love, we reach out to them. Or put another way, the only way our children and we, too, can acquire faith is to be part of the community of faith. Thus, we include our children in the believing community, and share with them our faith.

All the while, we strive to instill a sense of self-worth in our children. The mere fact that we take the time in the worship service to sit with them in that big sanctuary with all the adults present means more than words can fully express. It goes without saying (and surely the children perceive this) that they are deemed important. They have "worth" in the eyes of the church. And it is not just what is *done* to teach this self-esteem, but also what is *said*, reminding them that they are created in the "image of God." In essence, this is what Jesus taught and demonstrated, and the young among us need to know this as early as possible, to internalize it so that there is not recorded on their mental tapes the message, "I'm not OK!" For all too many, that negative message is already taped. That old tape needs to be erased, and a new message recorded: "I'm OK!" It is vitally important that we help our children have a good self-image. What an

10

opportunity we have! There are ramifications of salvation in all this!

It should also be noted that we convey an adverse theological message when we cancel the children's message on a given Sunday. Why? The question does not ask the theological pros and cons of doing or not doing these sermons, but instead it ponders the wisdom (for whatever reason) of "programming" the children out of "their time." Recently, a pastor told me that he never has a children's sermon on Communion Sundays. He went on to say that there are some special Sundays when there are just too many other things in the Order of Service. Hence, the children's sermon is simply omitted. But if we omit the children's sermon, especially after the children have grown accustomed to the idea that in the worship service they have a special time, we subtly send them a theological message that has negative portents. We are saying, in so many words, "You are not important all the time." This really made an impression on me the one and only time I omitted the children's sermon, having the children's despair communicated with downcast eyes, and sad faces, i.e., "We weren't wanted this morning." Now I find time for the children's sermon no matter if it be on a Communion Sunday, or a particularly crowded service liturgically. What we do (or do not do) does have theological implications!

Another concern pertains to the words we use. Words not only have a *say* but also a *sway* in our lives, all of which requires us to note carefully the effects our words may have on others. So, when we talk about God, for example, we do not want our children to think of God as a Male (even if spelled with a capital *M*), which the word Father connotes. To substitute the word Mother, as some have done on occasion in order to give equal time or balance, is just as problematic. Our difficulty is compounded because we do not have inclusive pronouns which make much sense to us or to our children. For too long we have allowed our language to be dominated by the male bias, with God's gender being thus assumed. How many of our children, especially our younger ones, think of God as an elderly grandfather with a long, white beard? The movie *Oh, God!,* with George Burns, did not help! A friend's child saw a look-alike in an old pickup truck stopped at a traffic light and exclaimed with great excitement, "There's God!" Much the same thing happened to me on the first day of Vacation Church School when a child (whose family had been attending for only a few weeks) said to me as I walked by, "Hi, God!" We want our children's faith perception to expand beyond gender, beyond anthropomorphizing God, beyond that of making God into a *super* man, or a *super* woman, or even a *super* human. The divine mystery is too great, too wonderful, too personal to be limited to one particular gender, as Brian Wren has written in his "The Song of Three Children":

> God is not a she,
> God is not a he,
> God is not an it
>   or a maybe.
> God is a moving,
> loving, doing,
> knowing, growing
>   mystery.[14]

One unfortunate side effect of noninclusive language is the masculine bias (often unconsciously accepted and assumed). The inference is that maleness is of higher value than femaleness, or put another way, that women have less importance than do men in the overall scheme of human life. Nothing could be farther from the truth! And yet, the myth persists in our male-dominated (chauvinistic) society. Yes, even the Bible has this gender problem, which we now understand when we consider that early society (see John 4:7–27). However, when we read the Bible again, carefully noting how Jesus reacted and responded to others, we see how inclusive he was with all peoples, particularly with women, when it was considered a taboo for a religious teacher, albeit a rabbi, to talk with women in public! Many see a divine intimation at work here. Granted, this is a subject on which some may (nay, will!) take exception, either because they are not yet convinced that inclusive language is a valid concern, or feel it is too hard or confusing to implement. New pronouns are needed! Thus, they resist language changes altogether. This is, however, a matter of utmost importance, for how we speak of God and how we relate to the opposite sex is of theological significance for us and our children. We need to be inclusive instead of exclusive. (More about this on pages 69–77.)

To do children's sermons right, I firmly believe that we have to begin as we have—theologically speaking. To go straight to the how-to's without considering what we have so far would be wrong. Before a good house can be built, a firm foundation must be laid. I hope what I have said helps to give a good start in doing this. We begin by responding to the inquiring spirits of our children and in giving the assurance that God seeks to be known even by the young in our care. My supposition is that children are to be loved and wanted by us (as they are already by God), that they have value and need self-esteem (which God provides and which we can also reinforce), that they are of importance in the community of faith (for the fuller expression of the faith which they can receive), and that they need to know how to think and speak of God which will in turn honor God and enhance life (hence, the importance of the words we use). Yes, each of us needs to continue considering the theological ramifications of all this—and not just on Sunday mornings and Saturday nights.

If the theology of children's sermons were to be summarized, the words of Jesus would say it best: "You shall love . . . your God with all your heart, and with all your soul, and with all your mind, and with all your strength. . . . You shall love your neighbor as yourself [Mark 12:30–31a]." God, others, and self, each loved in the proper way, constitutes the theology that undergirds the children's sermon.

Meanwhile, some practical questions keep a persistent pressure on our homiletical sensibilities, especially as we draw nearer and nearer to the time when we are to be "with the children." The how-to's are many (as we shall soon note)!

Before rushing on with the how-to's of children's sermons (and already we have been dealing with one aspect of this, i.e., the theological), another concern needs to be mentioned in passing that goes beyond the scope of this book, though not beyond what is required to do better children's sermons: child development. Take time, which will be some of the most valuable time ever spent, to read the works of several key thinkers in this area of study, e.g., Jean Piaget,[15] Lawrence Kohlberg,[16] James Fowler,[17] Erik Erikson,[18] Mary M. Wilcox.[19] In essence, the theological and the developmental considerations are the foundation stones needed before these sermons for children can be rightly constructed. How can we provide helpful children's sermons unless we do so with a sound theological understanding, as well as a perceptive awareness of how children learn?

How-to has not always been the most popular of queries. The problem? Fred B. Craddock explains:

How does one person communicate the Christian faith to another?

But that question itself already hinders us, arousing a widespread notion that threatens to abort fruitful discussion. The threat lurks in a general feeling about the word "how." "How" is for many an ugly word, a cause of embarrassment. There is a large opinion that "how" is to be found not among the prophets or the philosophers but among mechanics and carpenters. After all, does not "how" introduce methods and skills more appropriate to a course in driver training than to probing in the mysteries of ultimate reality? What has *skill* to do with the kingdom of God? SK [Soren Kierkegaard] sensed some of this condescension among the clergy and regarded it as a major cause for the decline in the quality of preaching. Perhaps no word among us has suffered more abuse than "how," not the honorable abuse of attack, but the humiliating abuse of inattention, disregard, slight. "How" has been made to stand out in the hall while "what" was being entertained by the brightest minds among us. *What* is the issue? *What* is the truth? *What* do we believe? *What* is being taught? Those are the worthy questions, and who would suffer the embarrassment of interrupting the discussion with, "But *how* can we . . . ?"

· · · · ·

Survey the devastation wrought by an arrogant dismissal of method in our churches, colleges, and seminaries. Countless young men and women, graduates of excellent schools of unquestioned intelligence and commitment, are paralyzed early in their

15

ministries because in those tasks that are ministry, in the only sense that really matters, they do not know *how*.[20]

Well then, no excuses needed for what follows! On with the how-to's.

Style! It is as *Webster's Ninth New Collegiate* defines, "a distinctive manner of expression (as in writing or speech)."[21] My style more often than not is autobiographical. Years ago, when I first began preparing children's sermons, I did what seemed natural, purchasing books of children's sermons. However, I soon realized that much of the material in those books was *not me.* Yes, there were some good and acceptable sermons in them, and I used them mainly as seed ideas. But using only books for ideas was not enough. Sundays were back-to-back. I needed more material, more ideas, with which to work. Once the usable sermons had been used up, I felt this panicky feeling in the pit of my stomach. Again, I would go through the books, looking for a sermon I might have missed. Then, one day a friend said, "Why not do your own *thing?*" "But how?" I asked. "Just speak to them out of your experience," he replied.

So, one Monday morning after a disappointing Sunday, and with this helpful comment in mind, I realized that using those other sermons, even the good ones, meant speaking to the children in the third person, which was too impersonal, too distant. If the children were to be reached, I had to be more personal, more direct. "Experience is the best teacher" is the thought that kept coming back to me. Then it occurred to me that the experience had to be mine (or ours—thinking of the children). Authors are wisely told that if they are to write a book, they need to write about something they know. The same goes for children's sermons! Thus, I look to my own experiences (and also those that may include the children) in order to illustrate what I say to the children about the faith of the church.

The danger in doing this, of course, is that of ego-tistically elevating the self too much, to where it sounds like, "What a great person I am; and if you will just listen, I'll tell you so!" No, the initial purpose, or premise, is really very simple, that of personalizing the message in the first person so as to create interest and ready listeners. Only if the children's interest can be captured will they really hear what is being said. Note how closely others listen when one says, "Let me tell you what happened when I. . . ." And there are hundreds of personal "hap-penings" from which one can draw. Yes, there are many autobiographical experiences, if only the homiletical po-tentials therein can be seen. They are there to be seen and used! The autobiographical style works well for me, and I recommend it to others.

Here is how I proceed (my working outline):

1. This happened to me; let me explain.
2. Avoid bragging.
3. Use a prop to help illustrate (depending on the timing desired, the prop may be shown at any time during the sermon).
4. Do not over-explain, keep it brief, avoid side-tracking and unnecessary details.
5. Transition: "This caused me to realize . . ." / "Has this ever happened to you? Well, if so, . . ." / "From this I learned . . ." / "This means to me . . ." / "Ah, this causes me to think of . . ." / "When I . . . , this thought comes to mind. . . ."

(Note: At times a transition need not be ob-vious, being instead a very subtle shift in voice or in just the normal flow of thought, thereby bridging the gap to the lesson intended.)

6. Share what I think this means.
7. KIS (Keep It Simple)!
8. Relate it on the children's level both theologically and biblically.
9. Reemphasize *briefly* the main point.
10. Then, conclude with a one-sentence prayer.

One side benefit of this style is that the children tend to identify with me more quickly. This allows me not to be just another adult talking *to them,* but instead I have shared my world *with them,* so to speak. This makes us friends, and friends are ready listeners.

An example:

It's in the Book

PLOP!

That's how this book sounded when it was dropped onto my desk. My secretary smiled when she did this, saying, "Here's your new phone book."

Has yours been delivered at home yet? . . .

BIG, isn't it? And heavy too! I'd guess it's about three pounds. Also, thicccck! How thick? Two inches! How many pages is two inches? Not counting the cover, that's 1,162! Every year it gets bigger because more and more people are moving to our area.

The first thing I did after picking it up and looking at the cover (which is yellow and white, because that's the color of the pages inside this book) was to check out what it says about us here at the church. Did they get our telephone number correct? Sometimes a mistake is made. In the yellow pages, under CHURCHES, I located us, and our number is printed correctly. Then, it goes on to tell more about our church, our time of worship, when church school starts, where we're located, other information, and, yes, even who the minister is.

Then, I turned to my personal home listing. My name and address are correct!

It's all in the book, our new telephone book.

But look at all those other names. Hundreds! No, thousands! They say there are about 300,000 people in our city, plus another 100,000 in our county, outside the city. Just think how many telephones there are out there!

Now, think of taking just one telephone book from each town and city the world over and stacking them on top of one another. How high would that be? I don't know. Surely it would be higher than we could see. Just think of all those people in our world!

And in all those books are names and names and names. When I think of all those many names, and that I know only a few of all them, this thought comes to mind: God knows each person by name listed in all those phone books. God knows everyone!

It's in the Book! In the Bible it says that God already knows us all, and well! How well? Very well! It says, "Why, even the hairs of your head are all numbered [Luke 12:7]." So, surely our names are known.

Not only does God know each of us, God also listens to each of us whenever we want to talk—pray. We'll never get a busy signal as we often do on the telephone, for God is never too busy to listen and to talk with each of us.

Let us pray.

Dear God: Thank you for knowing all of us and for listening to each of us when we pray. Amen.

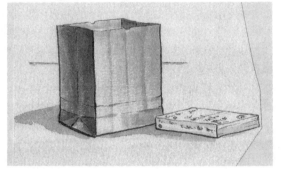

Of course, there are other styles. How dull we would be if we did it only one way. Even the pitchers in the major (and minor) leagues have three or four or maybe more different pitches in their plate offerings. As for myself, I have several, one of which I have already demonstrated, i.e., my bread-and-butter fast-ball, the autobiographical pitch. The others I use as "change-ups."

First, *biblical.* I once had a professor say to me, "If you don't know what to preach about, read the Bible." He was talking about adult sermons. However, the same holds true for children's sermons. Granted, much of the Bible, both in stories and in concepts, may well be over the children's heads. Never would I try to explain Paul's salvation theology, or the Old Testament minor prophets, or the book of Revelation. Also, I omit the "begats," most of the old histories, and all eschatological references. Even some of Jesus' parables were meant for the children's parents and not for the parents' children. Nevertheless, there is much in the Bible that can be used effectively.

Here are *some* examples of biblical props: figs; shepherd's staff; woven cloth; oil; pottery; needle; olives; yeast; scroll; fish; ram's horn; coins; picture of donkey; balances (scales); frankincense; lamp; fetters (leg shackles); idols (graven images); pomegranate; net; pruning hook; rainbow seen through a prism; and shield. Some imagination is required in order to see the homiletical lesson to be derived from each item, but it is there!

For example, figs. This was a food Jesus ate, and from that I led into God's goodness in providing us with food in abundance. I also added how today we need to share our abundance with others in the world in order to alleviate hunger, which is what Jesus wants us to do.

Another example is the shepherd's staff. With this I talked about the loving care of the shepherd for the lost sheep, or lambs, helping to pull them back to safety when they were in a thicket or at the edge of a deep ravine. Then, I talked about Jesus as the Great Shepherd, and of his love for us.

Yet another example is a scroll. I made it by cutting a strip from a brown bag and rolling this on two sticks. I showed the children what the Bible first looked like before it was made into a bound book. Instead of pages, it just continues on as it is unrolled. Then I showed them my Bible, bound one sheet after another, telling them that God still has a lot more to say to us in the Bible.

The important thing to remember is that we are not trying to make the children—at this young age—biblical scholars; rather, we want them to realize the value of this book and to have an awareness of the major truths (the "good news") found in it.

An example:

A Mitey Giver

Money. Let's talk about money. Who doesn't like to talk about money? Even Jesus did!

Once Jesus was in the temple, which was the main church of his day, and he sat down with his friends (called "disciples") just across from where people came to give their money. They didn't pass the offering plate as we do today. Instead, there was a box into which they dropped their money. The money then wasn't like paper money we have today; it was all coins. So, when the rich people tossed their money into the collection box, it made a lot of noise, and everyone could hear that they gave a lot. Yes, they had much to give, and everyone noticed!

But then along came a poor widow. She didn't have much money. Why was she poor? Perhaps she lived alone and had no way of making any money. Wha little she had may have been given to her. She had only

two copper coins, and these she dropped into the collection box. They didn't make much of a sound, so most people didn't even notice that she had given anything. But Jesus noticed!

And he said to his disciples that she had given more than all those rich people had. I can just imagine the disciples asking, "Why?" Here's how Jesus answered. The rich gave "out of their abundance," meaning that even after they had given, they still had much more left over. So, it didn't mean as much to them because they still had plenty. But of the poor widow, Jesus said, "she out of her poverty has put in everything she had, her whole living [Mark 12:44]." In other words, she gave all she had.

Before we go on, let me show you the kind of coin this poor woman put into the offering box.

It isn't very big. Do you see it? Here, let me hold it next to one of our quarters, which really shows you how small it is. It's called a "widow's mite." How much is it worth, or how much will it buy? I don't know. Not much, though! Maybe it would buy a piece of bread. And in today's money, surely it's not worth any more than our penny, and maybe less. What can you buy with a penny?

Well, that's the story and the coin. No, this isn't one of the very same copper coins she gave, but it's one like it. Here's what Jesus told his disciples, and also what he would tell us. When we give money to the church, it doesn't matter how much we give; rather, what counts is whether or not we are giving until it matters to us. You see, the rich gave a lot, but they had a lot. After they had given, they still had plenty. So, their gift of money didn't mean that much to them. As for this poor widow, she didn't have much, but she gave all she had. Oh, she could have kept one of the coins, I guess, though she

23

wanted to give both coins. Seeing this (and Jesus may have known who she was), Jesus said, "This poor widow has put in more than all those [others] [Mark 12:43]."

Why did she do this? Because she loved a lot! The others had a great deal, and while they gave a lot, they held back more of what they had because they didn't love as much.

Are we to give all our money? Jesus didn't say so. Rather, we are to give as much as we can, not just because we have a great amount, but because we love a lot. Even if we have little, and we still share as much as we can, that means a lot. This pleases Jesus, and God, too.

Remember, it's not how much we give that counts, it's how much we love to give that really matters the most. And the more we love the more we'll give.

Let us pray.
Dear God: Help us to give more because we love more. Amen.

Second, *biographical.* Biographies are a wonderful source for children's sermons. Each month there are the birthdays of notable people. In the month of February, for example, there are the birthdays of Lincoln and Washington, along with Lindbergh, Ruth (Babe), Dickens, Edison, Darwin, Galileo, Anthony (Susan B.), Anderson (Marian), Handel, Du Bois (W.E.B.), Caruso, Longfellow, to name just a few. From the life of each there is that *one* unique anecdote which can be the illustrative frame for a very "telling" message that conveys a Christian truth. Of course, this is not something to be done every Sunday, or even every month, but from time to time. For a change of pace, it is an effective approach to children's sermons.

An example:

Another Chance

Wednesday of this coming week, February 11, is the birthday of a very famous man: Thomas A. Edison. He was born a long time ago, more than a hundred years ago, in 1847.

He is remembered today because what he did still makes a difference, a *big* difference, in our lives. You see, he was an inventor. What's that? . . . Sure, some of you know. An inventor is a person who creates things never seen before.

In his lifetime he thought of and made 1,093 inventions (those are the ones that are recorded and protected by law), from the movie camera to improvements in the telephone (the part we talk into and hear out of), from the mimeograph (that's the machine which prints our Sunday bulletins) to the storage battery (we use batteries in our flashlights and toys). His most famous invention was the electric light bulb, the kind we use in our homes and here at church too. He worked hard and long on his ideas. But, at first, nothing seemed to work. How could he get that light inside that glass bulb?

Here, I have a clear light bulb to show you what the problem was.

No, this isn't the one he first made, but somewhat like it. See those little wires inside? They're called "filaments." They get very hot when electricity goes through them. When hot, they glow and give off light.

At first, he didn't know what to use to do this. He tried one thing after another, working for two years trying to find the right thing to use. At last he found it, but only after spending $40,000!

When it was completed, and after it had remained lit for more than forty hours, so the story goes, he gave it to his helper to put on the shelf for safekeeping. Guess what? His helper dropped it! And it broke! Did Edison get angry? Upset, yes, but not angry to the point of getting rid of his helper. Rather, he started over again, making yet another light bulb. Then, when it was finished, and tested for the second time, he called the same person for help, saying as he gave him the new bulb, "Would you put this on the shelf for safekeeping?" He did, without dropping it.

When I read this story about the light bulb, I thought about God and us. When we make a mistake, be it a big one or a little one, what does God do with us? Get angry and tell us we're not wanted anymore?

No! Instead, we're given a new chance to try again. That's right! That's what the Bible tells us, that when we make a mistake, or do a wrong, God loves us enough to give us another chance.

Let us pray.
Dear God: Thank you for always giving us another chance! Amen.

Third, *special days.* These are almost automatic. Who would want to omit Christmas and Easter? So it is for Thanksgiving! But then there are the Sundays of Advent, New Year's Day, Palm Sunday, Mother's Day, Father's Day, Valentine's Day, Independence Day, Halloween (or All-Saints' Day), Pentecost, Boy and Girl Scout Sundays, World Communion Sunday, in addition to all the local church days, e.g., Anniversary Sunday, beginning of Church School and Vacation Church School, and so on. Yes, special days, judiciously selected for use as a children's sermon context, are yet another avenue for us homiletically to travel.
An example:

Ears to Hear

It's back to school today!

Oh, I'm not referring to public school, which started a little over a week ago for most of you. Besides, you don't go to public school on Sunday. That would ruin a good weekend. Today is good because our fall Church School starts today. Even though you've been attending all summer, it's different today. Everyone is back from vacation. We're ready for our new classes.

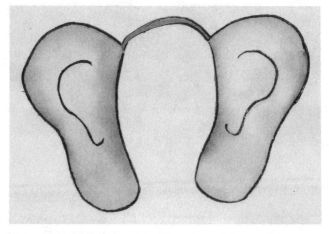

I can remember when I was your age, how excited I was on this day. And by the looks on your faces I can tell you feel as I once did. Guess what? I still get excited about this special Sunday in September. This morning is like the beginning of a new year.

Did you enjoy the special breakfast this morning? It was served in your honor by the Board of Christian Education. They do it every year—for you. They're excited too.

Now, when you go to the classroom this morning, you'll go to learn even more about God and Jesus. I want you to listen carefully.

When Jesus talked to people, he often said, "[Those] who [have] ears to hear, let [them] hear [Matt. 11:15]."

Have BIG ears! Oh, maybe not quite like, or as big as the ones I have to show you this morning, but almost. Have you ever seen twelve-inch ears?

Funny looking, aren't they? I put these big ears on just to remind you that one of the best ways to learn is to be a good listener. That's what I want to be—a good listener.

When your teacher tells you about God, listen carefully. Really, that is an important lesson you can learn at church.

When the Bible is read, listen closely, with this question in your thoughts, "What is this saying to me?" Believe me, the Bible has a lot to say to us and about us.

When your class discusses the ways to show love as Jesus taught, listen carefully.

Just perk up those ears all the time. Have BIG ears. Listen, listen, listen; learn, learn, learn.

That's why you've come to church this morning! Yes, to do as Jesus said. "[Those] who [have] ears to hear, let [them] hear."

Let us pray.
Dear God: Help us to listen and learn. Amen.

Fourth, *nature*. Folliott S. Pierpoint's hymn makes the point:

> For the beauty of the earth,
> For the beauty of the skies,
> For the love which from our birth
> Over and around us lies,
> [God] of all, to thee we raise
> This our hymn of grateful praise.

And that is the purpose of this type of children's sermon. In nature there are many illustrations, from leaves to fuzzy worms, from snowflakes to weeds, from birds' nests to flowers, from rocks to rabbits, from _____ to _____, and the list goes on and on. From each aspect of nature's selection, some good point can be highlighted. We need to express our thanks to God for making a world full of so much beauty. By exploring nature we are helping children to experience wonder, and to have an appreciation of science, which is really a study of God's handiwork. Children respond to their world naturally with eyes wide open, perhaps with more wonderment than do we adults who take so much for granted. Truly, this type of children's sermon can help them to think more about God in relation to the world.

An example:

It's a Buggy World Out There

Something is really bugging me this morning. I'm thinking about bugs. Our world is full of bugs—little ones and big ones, ones that crawl and ones that fly, pretty ones and ugly ones! We don't even know how many different kinds there are in the world, except to say that there are millions and millions and millions. That's more than I can count!

The other day I saw a bug I'd never seen before. It was light orange, had yellowish feet and a dark brownish head. It looked like a giant fly. It was beautiful. As I watched, I wished I could have caught it in order to look at it more closely. But then it flew away, and now I wonder if I will ever see one like that again.

Last Saturday I found a book at the library titled *A Dog's Book of Bugs,* by Elizabeth Griffen, with some wonderful drawings by Peter Parnall.[22] I like this book! Here's what the book's jacket looks like.

This is the way the book begins.

> FOR DOGS ONLY. This book is for dogs that like bugs. Not all dogs have discovered the bugging, bumbling, leaping, creeping world of bugs. But many have. They search out the ways of bugs with curiosity, with patience, and with joy. This book is for them.[23]

31

Oh, I thought this was written for children, but it says it is written for dogs. Dogs? I'm sorry I can't share all of this book with you. For now, let me show you just one page. It pictures a dog lying on the ground looking at the bugs all around. . . . And it says:

They fly . . . by. They zip and zoom where flowers bloom. They hop and leap into the air. They cling to things. They stop and sleep anywhere. They climb all the time. They crawl on anything at all. They fall. They burrow in the dark of logs and scurry in the hair of dogs.[24]

You know, God must have a lot of fun making bugs. What we need to do is to show a greater love of bugs!

This coming week I want you to stop bugging your parents (that's just a little joke) and start bugging the bugs. Here's how you can do it. In my brown bag, I have a yard of string for each of you. Some nice afternoon, take this string out to a grassy place and put it on the ground in a circle. Once you have done this, lie down on your stomach and look for all the bugs inside that circled area. Notice how many legs each bug has. Look closely at their wings. What shapes are they? Remember what you see so you can tell your parents, and so you can tell me next Sunday. While watching the bugs, keep this thought in your head: Look at what God has made! In the Bible we read, "In the beginning God created . . . [Gen. 1:1]," and, you know, God still is creating—even bugs! Glory be to God for legged and winged creatures!

Let us pray.
Dear God: Thank you for bugs! Amen.

Fifth, *lectionary*. Many find this a helpful way of developing their children's sermon ideas as part of the larger theme of the worship service, thus correlating that biblical discipline with a message for the children. From the scriptural theme for the morning, something of importance can be said homiletically to the children. As we know, the benefit of lectionary preaching (aside from the fact that it is a unison reading and preaching in larger Christendom) is to provide a good balance of biblical themes throughout the year. And this can keep even the "preacher" of children's sermons from overusing favorite themes.

Granted, to use the suggested lectionary lesson will require a very imaginative homiletical mind. But is it not the same for adult sermons? You may want to explore the possibilities here, along with the warning that if the lectionary readings for a particular Sunday do not come "alive" for you, do not force them. Look elsewhere (scripturally, or yet another type of children's sermon) for your inspiration.

An example (from the lectionary used by the United Church of Christ, 8th Sunday After Epiphany, Year C, with the Gospel Lesson from Luke 6:39–45, using verses 41 and 42):

Why do you see the speck that is in your brother's eye, but do not see the log that is in your own eye? Or how can you say to your brother, "Brother, let me take out the speck that is in your eye," when you yourself do not see the log that is in your own eye? You hypocrite, first take the log out of your own eye, and then you will see clearly to take out the speck that is in your brother's eye.

What a Funny Thought!

I've heard it said that we're not to put anything in our eyes smaller than our elbows.

Have you ever tried to put your elbow in your eye? Try it. . . . Not easy, is it? In fact, you can't. Come to think about it, that's a funny thought! Since no one can do this, why would anyone even talk about elbows in eyes?

No, elbows can't get in our eyes, but other things can. Usually, it's a finger trying to get out something that has gotten in, like a tiny, tiny speck of dirt. You've had that happen, haven't you? We all have. And that tiny, tiny speck of dirt feels like a big, big rock. It hurts! So, while trying to get it out, we rub, blink, rub, blink, rub, and blink. Warning: In doing this, we may do more

harm than we may realize, perhaps scratching our eye. The best thing to do when that something won't come out is to ask an adult for help.

Jesus once talked about things in our eyes. He said: "Why do you see the speck that is in your brother's [or sister's] eye, but do not notice the log that is in your own eye? [Matt. 7:3]."

What a funny thing to say! Think of it, a log in your eye! Just to show you how funny that looks, I have a log in my brown bag.

It's not a really big log. Have you ever seen anyone with a log in his or her eye? Well, here's how it looks. . . . I hear some of you laughing!

Oh, I didn't really put this log in my eye, it just looked that way. No, I don't want to hurt my eye. Anyway, it doesn't fit.

Jesus often made people laugh. To say something that is so silly only made those who heard it laugh. And the more they laughed, the more they remembered what he said. And that's why he said it this way.

Jesus was saying that if you see someone with a log in her or his eye, don't laugh but check to see if you have a log in your eye. What did he mean?

Let's say you know a person who says ugly things about your friends. So, you tell this friend to cool it, to not say those kinds of things. But you've forgotten, or overlooked, the fact that you've done the same. You too have said unkind things about others.

Question: What right do you have to tell your friend to stop bad-mouthing others if you are still doing it too? Another question: What about first stopping what you're doing wrong before you try to give this kind of advice?

Oh, it's so easy to see the wrongs others do. And it is so difficult to see how wrong—at times—our own actions are.

35

Jesus wants us, before we say anything about the wrongs others do, to first change our own wrong ways. Otherwise, to judge others without changing ourselves is being what Jesus called a "hypocrite" (Matthew 7:5). What's that? . . . It's a person who claims to be good, but then doesn't do what is good. We don't want to be accused of doing that, now do we? NO!

Let us pray.
Dear God: Help us to do something about our wrongs before we tell others about theirs. Amen.

Sixth, *storytelling*. Are not the best sermons ones with a story to tell? What is so valuable about this approach is that it is so natural. Many children have grown up with a storytime scheduled for them, be it at bedtime, or at the library, or at school. Furthermore, learning through stories is such a traditional way for us to pass on our cultural heritage. Why not, then, use the same methodology to convey our religious heritage?

What stories do we tell? There are many kinds. If we are creative, we can write our own. For myself, I dip into that vast supply of stories already available and use legends, fairy tales, nursery rhymes, fables (especially Aesop's), or children's storybooks. The great Russian storyteller, Kornei Chukovsky, writes: "The goal of story-tellers consists of fostering in the child . . . compassion and humaneness—this miraculous ability . . . to be disturbed by another being's misfortunes, to feel joy about another being's happiness, to experience another's fate as one's own." And he suggests that it is worth the time and trouble "to teach the child in his early years to participate with concern in the lives of imaginary people and animals, and to make sure that in this way he will escape the narrow frame of his egocentric interest and feelings."[25]

And, as I do this, I remind myself of steps to do this correctly: (1) finding an appropriate story; (2) remembering the time limitations to which I must adhere; (3) condensing the story accordingly; (4) rehearsing it, with special emphasis on good tempo, simplicity of words, and logical flow of thought; (5) using just the right amount of the dramatic—facial expressions and body movement; and, then (6) bringing the story to a fitting climax. If it is a good story, one worth telling, one that has a worthwhile message, I trust it and allow its meaning to surface without over-explaining. Yes, it is permissible to add a few comments at the end of the story to help the children perceive more of the intended meaning. But I do not underestimate their ability to make sense of the story.

Storytelling can be effectively used in the genre of children's sermons!

An example:

To Understand Fully

How many of you have stuffed animals at home? . . . What kind? . . . Do you have an elephant? . . .

I've brought a stuffed elephant, because I want to tell you a story.

This is a very old story, one the children of India love to hear.

Once there were six blind men who lived together. They lived in India, a land of many elephants. But they had never seen one. You see, they couldn't see, for as I said, they were blind. Oh, they had heard about this huge animal, though they still weren't sure what it was really like. So, together, they journeyed to the palace where they were given a chance to touch an elephant.

The first man touched the elephant's side and found it to feel like the wall of their home, saying, "So flat! An elephant is like a wall."

The second man touched the trunk and said, "How round and long! An elephant is like a big snake."

The next blind man reached out and took hold of the tusk and said, "How pointed it is! An elephant is like a spear."

The following man touched the elephant's leg and said, "How tall! An elephant is like a tree."

The next to the last man felt the ear and said, "How wide! An elephant is like a great fan."

And the final man took hold of the tail and said, "How thin! An elephant is like a rope."

They began talking about the elephant, and then they started to argue, with one saying the elephant is like a wall, another like a snake, another like a spear, another like a tree, another like a fan, and the last saying it is like a rope. Wall! Snake! Spear! Tree! Fan! Rope! And on they argued!

Then they were told by one who could see that none of them was right. Said he, "The elephant is a big animal. Each one of you has touched only one part. You must put all the parts together to find out what an elephant is really like."

They agreed, saying, "Each of us knows only a part. To find the whole truth, we must put all the parts together."

In the Bible, a man by the name of Paul said, "Now I know in part; . . . [1 Cor. 13:12b]." In other words, we never know it all. But this should never stop us from listening to what someone else has found out, for they may have something we need to hear if we are to know the whole truth.

Let us pray.
Dear God: We always want to be open to the whole truth. Amen.

Allow me to mention just a few more types of children's sermons. There is the *musical* type of presentation. If you play the guitar, banjo, harmonica, or some other instrument, or if you sing, this can be used effectively. The words of a song may have just the thought to be taught, and the music is like a teaspoonful of sugar that helps it go down, or which helps children remember. Or you may have a talent with *puppets.* It is amazing how readily children listen when a voice (and you do not have to be a ventriloquist) comes from the puppet. Or there is the casual type called *Question/Answer.* This can be tricky! When you are counting on the children to volunteer their comments, they may just clam up! Before you seek their comments or answers, it is necessary to get them excited about the subject. This takes experience, and an awareness of what is of interest to them. Or there is the use of *visual aids* including art, feltboard talks, and pictures—use of films or filmstrips is usually impractical because of lighting problems, logistics, and the time factor. Or there is the use of magic, but here I advise caution! If you are talented in this area, it may seem like a good thing to do, though for most it is an "iffy" proposition to master the sleight of hand. More problematic (and this is why I personally do not use magic in my homiletical bag of tricks) is the concern of what the children may deduce from it, i.e., that our religion is like magic. They could also get so caught up in the magical happening that the point to be made is relegated to insignificance, as well as being misinterpreted. My advice, if you insist, is BEWARE! But back to a type mentioned above!

An example (with hand puppet):

No Respect?

I have in my brown bag a friend.
Meet Freddie, the frog.
Oh, Freddie, meet some of my good friends.
     Fine looking young frog, wouldn't you say? Maybe
he's a little green around the mouth. Colorful, though!
He even has his name on his shirt. And look at how his
shirt is striped in the back. What about those blue
shoes? And isn't that some hat?
     Freddie, what do you have to say for yourself?
     What's that? Did Freddie stick out his tongue at us?
     I dare you to do that again!
     What?! Did you see what I saw?

41

Wait a minute. He's a frog. And frogs often stick out their tongues to catch flies and bugs. Right?

OK. Freddie, you can, if you must, stick out your tongue. But on second thought, there are no flies or bugs around here. So my advice to you is for you to keep that tongue inside your green mouth. Further, it's my suggestion, my insistence, that you not stick your tongue out at any of us.

When I was ever so young, I was taught that I should never stick out my tongue at others. And I can remember a few times when I did, feeling afterward that that wasn't right. Why? Because it is a sign of disrespect.

Disrespect? What does that mean? It means, in short, that we aren't showing the love to that other person or persons they deserve from us. It isn't the loving thing to do! And we are taught to love, yes, to love even those at whom we'd like to stick out our tongues.

Disrespect? Another way of explaining that big word is to say, "I don't care about you!" Or, "You're not worth my attention."

Listen to what it says in the Bible, "Let him [or her] keep his [or her] tongue from evil [1 Pet. 3:10b]." What do you think that means? It means that you're not to say something about someone else that isn't nice or true. Yes, at times we've said something we shouldn't have about others, and have had the same said about us. But just sticking out our tongues at someone can be a way of getting back without saying a word. Ever thought of it that way?

Respect! One way to explain this wonderful word is to say, "I will honor your right to be you." We read in the Bible: "Respect to whom respect is due [Rom. 13:7b]." That means doing as God asks of us, especially in the ways made known through Jesus. We are to love others. Let's do it!

Ah, let's allow Freddie to stick his tongue out—that is, if he really sees a fly flying around here—because that's his way of eating. But for us, . . .

Let us pray.

Dear God: Help us to show respect to one another. Amen.

There are many ways of presenting the message to our youngsters. Not all are workable for each of us. However, we never should limit ourselves to just one style. How boring that would be! How exciting for our children—and for us too—when we have a variety of children's sermons.

And we do want it to be exciting for our children in a learning way. Jean Piaget insisted that children be allowed to do their own learning. Granted, they need guidance; but when all has been said and done, it must be a firsthand instead of a secondhand experience. Of course, our children are not to be parrots, thinking only our thoughts and acting according to our dictates. Rather, the dynamics of the faith we share require us all to respond mentally, psychologically, and spiritually until it makes good sense to each of us personally. Otherwise, is our/their faith really real?

I try to keep this goal in mind from the moment I begin working on the sermon idea until I actually sit down with the children and say what I hope will be helpful to them. All this involves what I call the "Eureka Principle." Historically, this reminds us of Archimedes (287?–212 B.C.) who learned in a firsthand way, or by experience. He has become known as the "father of experiential science," for he tested his ideas by way of experiments. When he discovered the method for determining the purity of gold (volume displacement of water theory)— the truth of which came to him while taking a bath—he jumped out and ran naked into the street, shouting, "Eureka!" In Greek this word literally means, "I have found it!" Henceforth, this word has lived on in our language as an expression of triumph concerning a discovery. The most effective learning occurs when children say "Eureka!" Their way of saying it may be no more than simply, "I understand," or a look in their eyes, accompanied by a big smile, which suggests to me that the Eureka moment may have occurred! In order to bring this special moment about, I do several things intentionally.

First, *only one main point per sermon.* This admonition I have chiseled in stone. The logic of learning dictates it. If too many points are made, the children get confused. If they have really listened to many points, they are apt to select a less important one to take home. Of course, it is permissible to have several brief illustrations (or ways of demonstrating) in the sermon in order to explain the main point. But, remember, no more than one point.

Now, there is no way of telling how many different ways that intended point will be interpreted, for the point

44

will be different for each child, depending on the child's level of faith, experience, and intellect. Here it is important to check those brief illustrations so that they do not become separate points which would, or could, undercut the main point on which we wish them to focus their attention. The hope is that each child will be able to take home the main idea of the children's sermon. The task for us is to keep what is said clearly focused. If the children do not get the main point, they certainly cannot be expected to live it!

Second, *do not over-explain.* One of my professors in seminary (Edmund Steimle, noted preacher and teacher of homiletics at Union Theological Seminary in New York) would say to us, "Don't hesitate to use your blue pencil to delete all those unnecessary words." Shakespeare penned this truth thus, "Men of few words are the best men."[26] If we were to amend (in a more inclusive way) his first and last words, I think we would have an important thought to be remembered when it is time to present the children's sermon. Yes, the words need to be carefully chosen. What excitement awaits the children when they can put the two-and-two of faith together and get the four of greater awareness. It is exciting to watch this happen, or to hear from one of the children (usually one of the older ones) who wants to discuss the subject further. Not only are *they* excited by this Eureka experience when it happens, so am *I!*

Third, *ask open-ended questions.* How easy it is to make the children's sermon a monologue. I have even had some ministers tell me that they would never ask an open-ended question for fear of what they might get as an answer. I understand! Ask for an opinion, and you might get the unexpected, e.g., "I have a new dress on," or "We're going to Grandmother's house." Once I asked "What is a crèche?" and heard, "That's when two trucks

45

run into each other." However, it is important for the children to respond. Sure, I may not get the so-called "correct answer" each and every time, but that is not the main objective in this type of questioning. Their responsiveness tells me they are involved, and that is what really counts. (Also, they learn from one another's answers!) Some of my questions sound like this: "How do you feel about . . . ?"; "Have you ever . . . ?"; "Why do you think . . . ?"; "What is this . . . ?"; "Did you ever . . . ?" Again, my purpose is not to expect a "right" answer, or to keep pressing until someone comes up with it. In school the bright ones, more often than not, get all the strokes for knowing the "right" answers. But here the so-called "right" answer is not the most important consideration. Rather, we are all equal in God's eyes, and this is a good place to practice it! I use this questioning technique to promote involvement and thinking. Years of experience have validated its effectiveness.

But there is more! Allow the children to respond. Because of their Sunday-to-Sunday familiarity with me, they know their comments are welcomed. I listen to what they have to say, even though I am aware of our time limitations in this liturgical setting. I listen and then incorporate their comments, if possible, into what I am saying to them. With each response I respond, saying one of the following: "I agree"; or "Yes"; or "Right"; or "Good answer"; or . . . (the number of affirming answers are many). If the response from a child is "off the wall," I try to steer the conversation back to the subject at hand by saying something like this: "Well"; or "Hmm"; or "Interesting"; or "Here's another way to look at this." Never do I give a put-down, even if the response being considered is beside the point. I am careful not to get the congregation laughing at the response given, or even to laugh at my reply given to the child, for the child in question

46

may be easily embarrassed—and that is not my purpose. Granted, at times the congregation will laugh spontaneously, and when this happens I assure the child who caused the laughter that the adults are laughing "with" and not "at." How? If the child is seated near me, I give a hug, or a smile, or a word of encouragement, e.g., "I know what you mean"; or "That's happened to me too"; or "They're laughing because they like what you said." As the child responds, I warmly smile—with my eyes. Not only does this encourage responsiveness, it tells the children without my having to say it in so many words that I appreciate their expressing whatever they feel like saying.

Fourth, *do not moralize*. In other words, preach not! Here I am using the word preach in that sense which has given the art of preaching such a bad reputation. The problem here is that we are speaking to several levels of children's moral reasoning. Can we learn to write our material so we can trust the experience, rather than be obvious to the more advanced and meaningless to the lower levels? Difficult! Is this not the goal for which to strive? Of course, it is necessary to help our children to understand the right moral interpretation in a given situation. This can be done in a positive way, without having to moralize, thereby helping our young hearers better to understand ethically the difference between right and wrong. The concern is in how we do this. Who of us likes to be preached *at*? Maybe this is why some adults object to our talks with the children being called "children's sermons" (here, the word sermon is negatively interpreted). We adults do not like being talked down to, and neither do our children.

So beware of using obligatory words like "should," "ought," "must," and "have to." Our intent to effect a change in their young lives all too often is countered by a silent resistance. Such imperative, commanding, and demanding words need to be avoided. Let us not insult their youthful intelligence! It is much more successful to win their agreement than it is to force them to comply against their will. Our persuasion is love! It is amazing what positive reinforcement can do to shape their young lives.

Fifth, *stay within the children's experience.* When illustrating the point being made, I try to pull from those experiences to which they can personally relate, such as home, school, friends, and church. This helps to ground the message in the familiar, where they live. Also, because the time frame for the children's sermon on any given Sunday is limited, it is vital for the children to understand as quickly as possible what is being said. If I take them too far from where they "live," either intellectually or experientially, I may well lose them along the way. However, while this is true for the younger children, it is also true that the older children relate to the other experiences. On occasion, I like to give the older ones something more to think about, to experience, and let the younger ones stretch. This shows all of them that I expect a lot of them. Children are the greatest learners there are! I do not want to underestimate them! (Note point six, below.) But more often than not I keep them grounded with what they are most familiar, illustrating the meanings, or implications, being taught in ways they can readily grasp. From experience I know that this kind of "referencing" on their level of awareness is vital. And when I do not do this, or when I get too far over their heads, I know it before the sermon is over. They tell me without saying a word, with blank stares and restlessness. We have misspent the time with them if we fail to heed this experiential truth.

Sixth, *encourage the children personally to be (and do) more.* I try to interject just enough of a query that will cause them to question themselves ("How can I be—or do—more?") so they will seek answers which provide for personal accomplishment ("I can!"). Hence, growth, i.e., theologically, in a greater awareness of how they can better relate to God and to others. This requires a familiarity, a personal knowledge of and acquaintanceship with the children. How easy it is to make the children feel that they are just fine. This concept of growth does not want them to be too completely satisfied or dissatisfied with themselves. Rather, the encouragement ever so subtly suggests that they can be (and do) more than they are. Helping them to come to terms with this gives them a new level of awareness. When they do this, they have the joy of accomplishment. Then, it is necessary for another round of encouragement. In essence this is widening the horizons of what can be. The children will not speak of it this way, but we understand it to mean "growth." And is not this the hope for our children's sermons—not knowing how each child will grow, but ever seeking to help in that vital process?

Early in my ministry I shared with the children the story of the little red engine that could.[27] The other engines said they could not make it up the long, steep hill, and even this little red engine, the smallest of them all, thought much the same at first. But then it began to think that perhaps, just maybe, it could. So it started saying, "I think I can, I think I can, I think I can," until at last it did. Unfortunately, early in life, really all too early for all too many, our children have learned to think negative thoughts about what they were capable of doing and being. This really is unfortunate! However, this despairing state of mind can subtly be used positively. This is when we help the children become dissatisfied with their negativity, and they begin to doubt their doubts. Then, when paralleled with the positive, be it in achievements or personal behavior or in relating better with others, perhaps the desired change can occur ("I think I can, and I will!"). This needs to be applied in a faith context, and on their level of perception. Being aware of this growth theory, I work to inspire them accordingly.

"Eureka!" What a wonderful word! To have our children say in their own way this old Greek word, in essence, "I see," or "I understand," or "I believe," implying that the truth of the faith is more fully perceived by them, is the goal we strive to obtain. One truth learned leads on to yet another truth waiting to be understood and believed. That is what it is all about, and why we congregate together in and as the church to help one another in this "faithing" process.

An example:

Beyond My Reach

Question: Have you ever tried to reach for something and you couldn't quite get it? It was just beyond your outstretched fingertips? . . .

This happened to me the other day. The shelf was higher than I am tall, and I wanted something on the very top. Even by standing on my tiptoes, and by stretching my arm out as far as I could, I still couldn't get it. My thought was that that shelf was too high.

If only I had had what a friend gave me just yesterday. I put it in my bag this morning to show you. Have you seen one of these? . . .

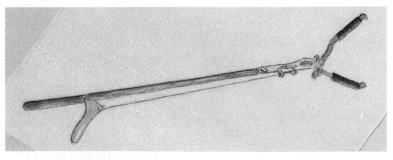

I'm not sure what it's called. Let's call it an arm-extender. Well, whatever we call it, it works!.

Here, let me show you how it works. As you can see, it has a handle that squeezes, and that opens and closes the pincers at the other end. Oh, I was going to show you how it works. Let me toss this wad of paper over there, just beyond my reach. No way could I reach it with just my arm alone. Look, this arm-extender helps me to reach beyond what I could do otherwise.

This arm-extender reminds me of something more. Are you unhappy at times because you would like to be better than you are?

Take sports, for example. Have you ever heard yourself say, "If only I could run faster," or "throw a ball better," or "hit the ball farther," or "jump higher"? And then to say, "If only I could, I'd be much happier"? What about your schoolwork? Have you ever said, "If only I were better at reading, writing, and math"? Or, maybe you've said to yourself, "If only I were not so messy, or loud, or late, or moody, I'd like myself more and so would others!"

You know, we all feel that way at times—unhappy with ourselves. And that's OK. Question: If we didn't at times feel unhappy with ourselves, or dissatisfied in how we were doing something, would we ever try to do better? I don't think so!

Do you think God made you and me to be less than what we are able to be? Hardly! So, God is always wanting us to be better than we are. It says in the Bible, "Do your best to present yourself to God . . . [2 Tim. 2:15]." I believe that God believes in us, meaning that we can do our best, that we will do better. When we begin to understand God's faith in us, that is when we grow on the inside, causing us each to say, "I can and I will do better than I have before!"

51

That makes God happy! We're reaching out to be more than we presently are. Just in reaching out, in trying harder, we are happier too.

Let us pray.
Dear God: We want to be better and to do our best. Amen.

Now, turning from this "Eureka Principle," we need to reach for more ways in which we can provide better children's sermons. Consider props.

Always a prop! There is something about a visual aid that complements the learning process. The eye and the brain do work together. The prop needs to be simple, easily handled, and within the scope of the children's experience. While the age range of the children varies greatly on any given Sunday, the visual configuration of a prop helps to focus their attention. It has been my experience that months later a child talks about a prop I used in one of my sermons, and then recalls the point of the sermon! Or I will hear from a parent, as I did one Easter. The prop used that Sunday was a closed fist with the thumb sticking up, cut out of colored posterboard, with the fist and thumb outlined with magic marker in a pop art style. One was given to each child. The point was that the people who killed Jesus had turned thumbs down on him (prior to this we had talked about what it means to turn thumbs down as well as up), but God had given the thumbs-up sign, meaning that Jesus would live again, thus the Resurrection. The father reported to me that his son (five!) had told his visiting grandmother, who had not heard the sermon, what had been said by me, almost verbatim! Using the prop, he "preached" the sermon!

What about handouts? On occasion I have a prop which the children can take home. Some of the take-home props I have given have been: plastic bags of mung beans (with instructions for growing); gold-ore rocks (from the tailings of an abandoned gold mine); friendship rocks (little rocks that have a hole in them, through which I put a string); one-inch squares of sandpaper; pretzels; palm branches; paper butterflies; paper shamrocks; fortune cookies (homemade); badges (DUO—"Do Unto Others"); cardboard crèches (with straw, all in plastic bags); flower seeds; big buttons (one read "My Mom Is The Greatest"). And there have been more! Oh, how they love handouts! But in doing this, it is wise to think ahead as to how best to hand out these kinds of props systematically, or otherwise you will be mobbed. I often have the props on a large piece of posterboard, each one attached with a curled piece of masking tape for easy distribution. At times I have teenagers, or even some of the children, help. The purpose for handouts is to help the children remember what was said.

Here are some of the props I have used:

Camera	Box of Cheerios
Suggestion box	Dictionary
Blueprint	Magnifying glass
Deck of cards	Dominoes

Softball	Banana peel
Fishing pole	Security blanket
Gloves	Thermometer
Loaf of bread	Hole punch
Suet	Wastebasket
Catalog	Bird nest
Tube of toothpaste	Fossil of a fish
Music box	Razor
Yo-yo	Piggy bank
Fingernail	Frisbee
Wig	Pillow

An example (taking my pillow as a prop):

Be Awake!

It's morning, isn't it? Time to wake up. Right? But, oh, how nice it is to keep your head on the pillow and sleep just a little longer.

Do you ever sleep in? . . . Fun, isn't it? Fun, yes, that is, until Mother or Dad comes and says in a very convincing way that it is time to wake up and get up.

By the way, I just happen to have my pillow in my brown bag.

This is my favorite pillow. I guess it would have to be my favorite since it's the only one I have. I love it. And is it soft! Just right for me. Inside it are tiny goose feathers. Those are the softest of all. So, if I want to shape it to fit my head just so, I can make it even more comfortable. It's not like those pillows that have springy foam rubber in them. Those kinds of pillows I don't care for, for they never seem to fit my head. But this one does!

For this occasion (you see, my pillow has never

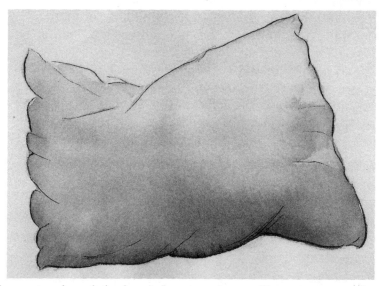

been to church before), I put a clean pillowcase on it. It smells so fresh and clean.

Do you mind if I Zzzzzzzzzzzzz. Oh, excuse me, I was talking to you, wasn't I? I better wake up and . . .

You know, sleeping is a big part of life. That's the way God planned it. We'll all sleep about a third of our lives. Or, think of it this way: There are twenty-four hours in a day, and we sleep about eight hours; that's a third of the time sleeping. But that's OK. Our bodies need the rest. Sleep is important, but only at the right times—at night, or that short nap during the day for some additional rest.

Yet, all our time isn't to be spent on the pillow. Rather, most of our time we're to be awake.

Are we sleeping when we need to be awake? Awake to how we can be more loving? Oh, that doesn't mean we're laying our head down on a pillow and snoozing away. It could mean that we're not really doing what we need to be doing. Maybe we're daydreaming, and not paying attention. The problem is that then we can't really be as caring as we need to be. It is as if we're asleep to what's around us.

In the Bible I read this about being awake: "So then let us not sleep, as others do, but let us keep awake [1 Thess. 5:6]."

I take this to mean that (except for an occasional nap) we're to be awake all day long to how we can be doing what Jesus wants us to do—all the good we can for others.

BE AWAKE!

Are you awake? If not, I'd say to you, "Awake! Consider how you can be loving each and every day."

Let us pray.

Dear God: Thank you that we can be awake to the ways of love. Amen.

Where do props come from? I find myself surrounded by them everyday. Let me cite three examples. (1) One day as a barber was cutting my hair and it fell into my lap, I thought that this might serve to illustrate the problem of looks and beauty. While it is good to look nice, what matters to God is how beautiful we are on the inside, how loving, kind, and good we really are, despite what we look like on the outside (title of this sermon: "More Than Looks"). (2) I brought my tissue box one Sunday, and blowing my nose, told the children that I had been sick with a cold. Then I told them that when I was sick I did not feel very religious. I felt so "augh!" about everything that God seemed far away, not at all near. But—I continued—God is always with us, near us, in spite of how we feel (title: "Ah-choo"). (3) I picked a black-eyed Susan and brought it to church. As I pulled off the petals, I talked about being loved, saying, "She loves me, she loves me not," etc. But I told the children that when we talk about being loved by God we do not have to do this, for we have a better way of knowing that God loves us, i.e., Jesus, the Bible, parents, friends (sermon title: "The Flower Test").

One of my favorite ways of finding props (hence, sermon ideas) is reading books of illustrations, or finding illustrations in books. Then I think about how to use that illustration with the children in the form of a prop. For example, while thumbing through a copy of *The Ministers Manual,* here was a quote by Dr. Ralph Sockman:

> Jesus was no ruthless iconoclast. He possessed a historical perspective which made progress toward the new by keeping track of the past. As the rearview mirror on a car enables the driver to see what is behind without taking his major gaze from the road ahead, so Jesus kept in view the old laws of Israel in order that he might make better headway toward the new laws of the kingdom of heaven. For, significantly enough, it is when we would turn left that we most need to see the road behind us. Likewise, in our social progress it is our "left" turns which need to be

safeguarded by historical perspective lest in trying to move toward the new we be run into by some old error coming down the road bearing a modern license plate.[28]

As I read this quote (not to the children, but in the privacy of my study), the rearview mirror jumped out at me, and another children's sermon was born. Here it is:

On Looking Back

In my brown bag I have a mirror.

Let's see how I look. I don't think I look that bad. Oh, that isn't why I brought this mirror, just to look at myself. I can do that at home, when I shave. And this

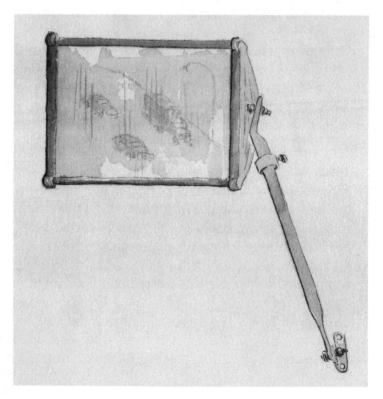

isn't even that kind of mirror, now is it? No, this isn't the kind you have in your bathroom, or even the kind you'd carry in your pocket or handbag. What kind of mirror is this? . . .

From a car? No, from a pickup truck. A friend took it off his own pickup for me to use this morning. Now that's a real friend!

Tell me, what is a rearview mirror used for? . . .

Right. It's to look behind you when driving a car.

Are any of you driving a car these days? What am I talking about? You don't have your license yet!

Think how unsafe it would be if you were driving down the road (let's pretend you can drive a car), and you wanted to know who was behind you. So, you turn your head . . . all the way around to look. What have you done? You've taken your eyes off the road in front of you. And that could mean danger to you, to others, and to your car. You see but you don't see. Yes, you see what's behind you, but by looking that way, you fail to see what's ahead of you. If you do this too much, you won't be driving very long. And I'll most likely be seeing you in the hospital. It's dangerous!

No, this mirror is to help make you a safe driver. With just a quick glance into it, you can see what's in back of you without turning your head. This mirror is for your safety, the safety of others, and for the safety of your car.

But I can't look in this mirror without also thinking how much this is like life. If we only look back, without also looking ahead, we could crash. By this I mean that we keep saying yesterday was more fun than today, so I'm going to keep looking back to then. So, in our thoughts we're thinking only of how much fun it was, and not seeing how much fun there still is to come. Yes,

59

it is OK to look back, to remember the way it was. That's why God gave us all the ability to remember. But we need to watch out, for too much looking back can cause us to fail to see what is ahead of us. I believe that the best is always ahead of us. Think of it this way, your life is ahead of you, not behind you.

Are we to forget what is behind us, what has happened to us in the past? It says in the Bible, "Forgetting what lies behind [Phil. 3:13b]." Should we do that? No! The person who wrote that (his name was Paul) meant only that we should forget the wrongs we've done when once we're forgiven, and not let the wrongs in our past keep us from looking ahead to a better future. He went on to say, "Straining forward to what lies ahead, I press on . . . [Phil. 3:13b–14a]." Most certainly we are to be excited about what is ahead of us.

Let us pray.
Dear God: Help us to know when to look ahead and when to look back. Amen.

I have the good fortune of having several friends who find a joy in providing prop possibilities. Sometimes I suspect they pass along their suggestions just to see what I will say to the children in reference to these props. At other times they really feel they have just the right prop, if not the best ever found. I make no promises to use what they offer, but I take their suggestions seriously. Basically, they want to help me, and God knows I need all the helpful ideas I can get! In the meantime, the prop may stay in the corner of my study for weeks before I see how to use it. Their involvement is greatly appreciated! Not only is it fun, but also stimulating and helpful.

An example (thanks to Sam and Nance Mc-Cullough):

Pain and Cane and Explain

Yesterday evening, I got a pain in my left knee. It really hurt! Why this pain? I didn't fall, or hit my knee some way. It came on unexpectedly. I had been sitting in a chair for about an hour, and when I got up—WOW!

Have you ever had a pain in your knee like that? Maybe you're too young. Do you think I'm getting too old? . . . How old do you think I am? . . . Well, I'm old enough to have an unexplained pain in my knee. And it was still there this morning when I climbed out of bed. You see, it only hurts when I stand on it, or move it while walking. When I'm sitting, or lying down, I'm OK. Isn't that the craziest thing? Maybe tomorrow it will be better. I sure hope so! But if it gets worse, I may have to use what I have in my brown bag. Some friends gave me this just last week.

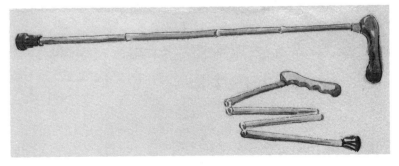

A cane. See how it works. It's collapsible! Have you ever seen a cane like this one? I hadn't until just recently. I just hope I don't have to start using this cane all the time. That thought really pains me!

But I think of others who do have to use a cane. Why? It could be that their knee, or knees, were hurt in an accident and the cane helps them walk, as well as stand. Or, it may be that they are getting older and the joints in their legs, and especially in their knees, don't work as well as they used to. That was one of my first questions about my pain, "Am I getting old faster than I think I am?" (By the way, getting older, or old, doesn't mean you'll get pains in your knees and then have to use a cane. But it could happen.)

Not only do I think of our older friends who use canes, but also others who have to use crutches, or walkers, or even wheelchairs. My first thought usually is to feel sorry for them. But no, they don't want our pity.

Whether they be disabled or hurting, or slower-moving because of increasing age, just remember that they need our "Yes"—our encouragement—instead of our "No"—our discouragement. Isn't that the way we'd like to be thought of and treated if we were in their place?

So, when you see people using a cane, or a walker, or crutches, or a wheelchair, remember that, despite their problem, they still have a lot to offer us all. They're still people who can do more than we may first think possible.

The main idea is this: No matter our problem, or problems, all of us still have a lot more we can do if just given the chance. We all just want to be fairly treated.

Remember the golden rule: "As you wish that [others] would do to you, do so to them [Luke 6:31]." That's the loving thing to do.

Let us pray.

Dear God: Help us to help others to do all they can. Amen.

(P.S.: What a coincidence! The pain I experienced in my leg, though temporary—lasting about a week—was real. Sam and Nance had no way of knowing that this pain and their prop would come together so soon in a children's sermon.)

Allow me a personal footnote, or "bagnote." In the preface of my first book of children's sermons, *The Brown Bag,* I noted what I consider an important point in using a prop.

> Ever since I began preaching sermons for children I have used a brown bag to carry the prop used in illustrating each sermon. Quite by accident, it has become my trademark. I am often asked when I arrive at church on Sunday morning with my bag in hand, "What do you have in your bag this morning?" My reply is always the same: "Wait and see." The advantage in using the bag is that it builds a

sense of anticipation in the children, causing them to be ready listeners before I have ever said a word.[29]

No, it does not have to be a brown bag, or even a green bag! A neighboring pastor uses a box. Anticipation is the rationale. Like a well-timed joke, or a well-told story, I want the prop to be employed at just the right time—and no sooner!

Remember: Children learn concretely. So, when we use props, we need to be careful how we use them. Iris V. Cully, in her book *Christian Child Development,* gives an illustration of the difficulty.

> For example, a minister sees a connection between a map and a Bible: each is a guide. Now children can understand what a map is, but they cannot see how the Bible is like a map. They watch it being used when the family is traveling. They can further understand that the Bible is a book that tells about God, and that it tells how God wants people to live. But the connection between traveling to grandparents' house and traveling the road that God sets is a confusing one.[30]

In my correspondence with Professor Cully about this, she indicated that there is a difference, a big difference, between saying something is *like* this or that (when in fact they are not the same) and saying that something *reminds* us of something else (when in truth it can). She noted, "Objects are useful reminders—that is one of the ways children learn."[31] The problem is, as she noted further, "They do not transfer an abstract idea from an object, because children think concretely." Thus to try to push children, before they are ready, into the reasoning of abstracted analogies—e.g., a rainbow is a sign of hope in the midst of a storm, or a mustard seed is like the "king-

64

dom of God," or an Easter lily tells us of Jesus' resurrection—is a waste of time. The world of the child is much more concrete and direct. Rather, the use of an object should remind the children of something, and then lead into a simple truth that can be internalized with their own experiential understanding.

An example (again, thanks to Nance and Sam Mc-Cullough):

Bananas in Our Ears?

First, I want you to close your eyes until I tell you to open them.

[While their eyes were closed, I put on a head band that has a plastic banana on each side.]

OK, open your eyes.

Did you ever hear about the man who had bananas in his ears?

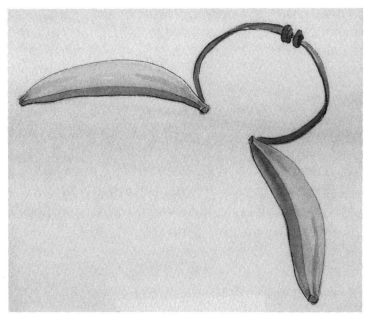

What did you say? I can't hear you! You see, I have bananas in my ears. Again, I ask you, did you ever hear about the man who had bananas in his ears? What did you say? I can't hear you, for I have . . .

Oh, sorry, I can't hear you, because I've got bananas in my ears. Let me take them out so I can hear what you're saying. Have you ever heard of such a man? . . .

You know, we do often have trouble hearing one another because we have bananas in our ears. Oh, not real bananas, or not even fake ones like these some dear friends gave me a couple of weeks ago. You know that real people don't have real bananas in their ears, unless they are acting silly.

But we do act like we have bananas in our ears a lot of the time. By this I mean not really hearing what others are saying to us.

For example, someone might say to us that he or she needs help. We nod our heads as if we've heard, but then we don't do anything to help. It's as if we didn't hear at all. Why? Oh, there may be any number of reasons why we don't really hear. Could one reason be that we're thinking more about something else we want or need instead of really listening?

Or, let's say someone says something to us for our own good—like good advice. It could be that we're not as sharing with others as we could be, or that we're making a pest of ourselves around others, or that we need to talk with a softer voice. But we don't want to hear this advice. We act like we have bananas in our ears, bananas that keep us from hearing what we need to hear for our own good.

Or, once more we hear what we've been told ever so many times in this big room, the sanctuary—to love

66

God in *every* way possible. Have we? Or, do we have bananas in our ears?

Are we talking about real bananas? Of course not!

When the help others ask for from us is not heard, or we don't listen to people we need to listen to, or we don't love God as we've been taught, what are we to do? My suggestion is, let's get those self-grown (pretend) bananas out so we can really hear.

There are some words in the Bible that come to mind when I think about bananas in our ears, "And the ears of the deaf unstopped [Isa. 35:5]." Bananas make us deaf, or hard-of-hearing, when they are in our ears, and we need to have our ears unstopped. So, get the bananas out!

Let us pray.

Dear God: We want to listen as Jesus taught—with love.

Amen.

So, we have the idea, and the prop, now what? How do we proceed? When I arrived at seminary, my first homiletics professor was the famed preacher of Christ Church (Methodist) in New York City, Dr. Ralph Sockman.[32] I shall never forget his comment: "Now, for the next ten years, I want you to write out your sermons in a manuscript form." His logic was that if we did, this would set our method of preparing sermons—ten years can instill a deeply ingrained habit. I have continued to do so since, even with children's sermons.

I know there are those who work their thoughts out in different ways. Some can put them together in their heads, and they come out with great eloquence and clarity, which is a unique gift. Others can jot down a few notes and go from there with ease. All of us must find our own way, our own method of preparation that best suits our temperament. However, manuscripts cause me to be intentional in the *what* and *how* that is said to the children. This means choosing my words carefully (words the children can relate to); checking the sequential flow (whether or not my thoughts logically connect); selecting the most meaningful illustrations (ones that are simple and direct); avoiding moralizing (omitting all those obligatory words); and gauging the length (approximately five to six minutes).

Note: The manuscript is for my preparation only! I do not take it—or notes—with me when I sit down with the children. Once written and rehearsed aloud several times, I have it well in mind. Then I am ready! At first, when I started doing children's sermons, I used a 3×5 card with an outline on it. If you feel uncomfortable at first going mentally "cold turkey," you may want to use this crutch. However, keep working toward the time when you can speak extemporaneously.

Further note: The process of writing, whether it be done with a pen, a typewriter, or a word processor, requires careful honing. E.B. White, writing on style, suggests what is required of us: "Revising is part of writing. Few writers are so expert that they can produce what they are after on the first try."[33] As I revise my manuscript (often three or four or more times), I continue to add or delete words and phrases, even sentences if that helps the logical and clarifying flow of the thoughts for the children. The question I continually struggle with is whether or not I have said enough to have explained fully enough, while not over-explaining. As for the problem of deletions, the motto I use is: "When in doubt, take out." Here is a thought I have mentally tacked up above my desk, again taken from E.B. White's chapter on style in the book *The Elements of Style,* a book I would not be without: "Remember, it is no sign of weakness or defeat that your manuscript ends up in need of major surgery. This is a common occurrence in all writing, and among the best writers."[34]

An example? No. I will leave that to you. Further, when I finish a manuscript, it looks like I was trying to see if a red felt-tipped pen worked, leaving red marks all over the pages. I am quite unlike Mozart, who reportedly composed without having to make any corrections. In fact, I have yet to meet anyone who, like Mozart, does not have to do some rewriting. Earlier I mentioned that Dr. Steimle advised us on the use of a blue pencil when the first draft had been completed (and the same goes for the second and third drafts), producing careful honing. I prefer red. The intent is the same—a better sermon!

When working on a manuscript, i.e., honing/revising it, I try to be very careful about inclusive language. This has become an important consideration in the church and in our society. Like many others, I became sensitive to this issue ever so slowly, in part because no one (until a few years ago) really called me to task on it. Soon after my first book of children's sermons was accepted by the publisher (1977), the editor called to talk about it. She helped me to see that in *every* sermon, on *every* page, the masculine language stood out like a *sore thumb.* A corrected manuscript was soon in the mail! This, plus having a few colleagues raise the issue with me (one was a woman minister in her seventies), caused me to be converted to inclusive language. On an even deeper level, I since have realized the power of words, and how they can put down or exalt ever so unintentionally. My complaint to the editor still stands, when the language is in reference to God: "We need some acceptable pronouns for God!" What John Westerhoff wrote in his book titled *Will Our Children Have Faith?* I too affirm, sensing his struggle as mine:

> (I am troubled as to how to speak of God. He/she seems right, but perhaps only the word God should be used. I do not want to distort the nature of God nor ignore the justice due those who are left out and estranged by masculine language.)[35]

Or, here is another comment that has caught my eye and has prompted some personal pondering:

> A society in which sexual or racial discrimination is traditional will employ a language in which that bias is reflected. Changes in the language to correct such bias can both reflect changes in the society and at the same time produce such changes. If women and ethnic racial groups are to be acknowledged as full human beings and partners with men and white

people in the fullness of Jesus Christ, we must, as a church, confront language bias and as a church act as a continual force for human liberation, salvation, and healing. Change occurs slowly and only through the commitment of the many who begin to demonstrate new vision and new behavior. Such commitment will produce new ways of speaking about the movement of God in history as that power which has liberated and freed us all from the bondage of the past.[36]

What about the Bible and inclusive language? That is more difficult, for many biblical words *seem* so divinely fixed, so authoritatively unchangeable, not even an iota or dot is to pass from the standard usage. This argument would be more convincing if there were one, and only one, translation. But since the turn of the century there have been many English translations of the scriptures. In comparing a few, it is obvious that the Word as expressed in the original Hebrew and Greek has found expression with a variety of word selections. It has been said that every translation is really a mistranslation, for the original language cannot be rendered 100 percent accurate in all instances. One leading biblical scholar, Walter Brueggemann, has stated that every translation is in essence a paraphrase, with the translators trying their best to choose the nearest, or most appropriate, contemporary words to relate as accurately as possible what was originally written.[37]

Well, when using the biblical text, why make all this fuss over inclusive language? Here are two important considerations: to ensure a God-intended dignity for women and to provide a larger view of God. I, for one, make changes when necessary; for example, changing the pronoun he to "God" (when God is being referred to), or inserting a "she" along with "he" (when the "he" was intended to mean both men and women), or in the latter context inserting "they" in the place of both "she" and "he." Or again, altering "sons of God" to read "children of God." Never would I intentionally change (and I hope I never have unintentionally!) the meaning of the passage used, but I do try to make it more meaningful for all who are listening to what the scriptures are saying. When making inclusive changes in my manuscript, I still use the editorial device of putting all emendations in brackets.

Further, in my writing and speaking, if the pronoun can be deleted, I do so (e.g., "A Christian is someone who feels he is asked by God to love others" becomes "A Christian is someone who feels asked by God to love others"). Perhaps an article can be substituted for the pronoun in question (e.g., "Every Christian is asked by God to show her love for others" becomes "Every Christian is asked by God to show a love for others"). Writing in the plural often helps to solve the problem of the "generic" *he* (e.g., "A good Christian is a person who loves because he loves God" becomes "Good Christians are persons who love because they love God").

These are some of the ways I continue to struggle to be more inclusive in my use of the scriptures, as well as in all that I write and say.

Yes, I strive vigorously to be inclusive when I speak to the children, and I encourage you to do the same. Why? Allow me one more quote from the above-mentioned publication on inclusive language guidelines.

It has been stated: "We cannot deny that language both reflects and shapes understanding, behavior, and faith. It is a tool created to facilitate the way in which we relate to each other, to our culture and to our past, present and future. Language is, and must be, a living tool which changes and develops as our understandings and knowledge expand. Our theology should shape our language rather than being shaped by it."[38]

An example (or examples, for in the following sermon there are many noninclusive problems. Circle them as a way of testing your inclusive awareness. Then note the following corrections of these noninclusive difficulties, with the lines numbered for easy reference):

Chew on This

1   Boys and girls: How are your teeth this morning?
2   Why ask about teeth—and of all places, in church
3 on Sunday morning?
4   Teeth are important! That's why we brush them,
5 why our mothers remind us to take special care of them

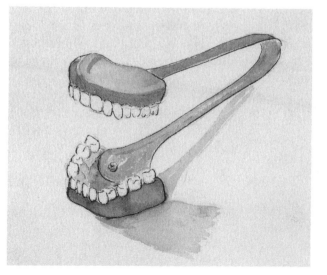

6 by seeing the dentist. He wants our teeth
7 to stay healthy. If you agree with him, and with me,
8 move your tongue across your teeth in a happy way.
9 Silly? Not really. We often get too busy to think about
10 our teeth, even when we're brushing.
11   Smile. Show me your teeth by smiling. . . . Beauti-
12 ful! Oh, I saw some teeth missing. But at your young
13 age new teeth will soon fill in the gaps. Don't worry.
14   Here are some teeth.
15   You laugh? I also laughed when I first saw them.
16 It's a set of man-made teeth—plastic—on the end of
17 serving prongs. What will man think of next?
18   Look at how they're shaped—for eating. We have
19 to eat to live! So, God planned for all mankind to
20 have a set of teeth. Sure, a small baby doesn't have
21 teeth, at first, but soon he will.
22   Look again at these fully grown teeth, and what
23 God has done. He made the front ones to cut and chop,
24 and the back ones to chew. And they all work very
25 well, every day.
26   Wait a minute. It doesn't work that well for every-
27 one. Here I'm not thinking of those who are having
28 trouble with their teeth, perhaps a toothache or having
29 to wear false teeth. Those are not happy thoughts.
30 But here I'm thinking of the use of teeth in chewing
31 food, and of the many people in the world who do not
32 have enough food to really use their teeth. How sad!
33   Many boys and girls, many men and women, go to
34 bed hungry each night. We here may not know them by
35 name, but we've been told that many have less food than
36 they need.
37   The problem isn't God's fault. In the Bible we read:

38   Thou dost cause the grass to grow
39   for the cattle,
40   and plants for man to cultivate,
41   that he may bring forth food from
42   the earth, . . . [Ps. 104:14]

74

43   You see, there is enough food in the world to feed
44 every man, woman, and child each and every day. However
45 this food in abundance doesn't always get shared as he
46 would have it to be shared.
47   We, in this church, have a big job to do. No, we
48 can't feed every hungry person in the world—all by our-
49 selves. There are too many of them, and too few of us
50 here. But we need to do all we can for as many as possible.
51 Some of you boys and girls are doing that already. From
52 where I sit, I can see bags of groceries some of you and
53 your fathers and mothers have brought to share with the
54 hungry. And some of you have even given money—pennies,
55 nickels, dimes, and quarters, even dollars—to buy more
56 food for the hungry in Africa. Also, I know that other
57 sister churches are helping, too, as are many men of
58 good will.
59   This is what Jesus wants us to do. It's what his
60 heavenly Father, and our God, wants, too, or else why
61 would he have given us all teeth?
62   Chew on this, which is another way of saying that we
63 need to think about how we can help. That's what I plan
64 to do. And when we do this, not only will the hungry use
65 their teeth, they'll also show their teeth with a big
66 smile. If only we could see that! God will!

67   Let us pray.
68   Dear Father: We want to help the hungry.
69 Amen.

Here are my correcting comments on the above lines:

1:    Why "boys" first? This makes "girls" second, a
      subtle put-down. Instead, say "Children."
5:    Are our mothers the only ones concerned about
      our teeth? Fathers need to be mentioned too.
6:    He? There are women dentists!

75

7:	Same problem.
16:	"Man-made" should be deleted. This subtly suggests that men are the ones who make things, leaving out any consideration of women. Some adults may argue that "man" is a generic term, meaning both men and women. But the children may not hear it that way, taking more literally what is said.
17:	Same problem.
19:	Ditto.
21:	The pronoun he excludes the girls. Must this be a boy about whom we are talking?
23:	Is God a male?
33:	Same problem with the "boys" being first and also the "men" being first.
40ff:	Question: Is it permissible to change the biblical word from "man" to "humans"? I do it if it doesn't then change the biblical intent and sense, all because I personally feel this inclusive consideration has merit. If written today, with this new understanding of words, surely the psalmist (Ps. 104:14) would concur.
44:	All people are mentioned, but again why "man" first? Why not just say "everyone"?
45:	Again, is God a male? We have used "he" enough over the years in reference to God that most of the children think of God as such.
51:	Problem already noted (lines 1 and 33).
53:	Why not just say "parents"?
57:	Why must a church be called "sister"? I know it has been so called for a long time, but does it

make any more sense than to call it "brother"? That sounds funny! Just omit it.

57: Are only "men" for good will? Women are too!

60: Yes, even Jesus spoke of his "heavenly Father," and in one sense I want to be able to do the same. But I hesitate to do so too often with the children for fear they may translate this into God being a Male Parent. I am perhaps a bit more cautious on this since I recently was told by my teenage daughter that her friend confided that when she was a small child she was sure the heavenly Father looked just like me! Alas! Certainly the children will hear "Our Father" when we pray together the prayer Jesus taught, and I am not in favor of changing this. However, I want the children to think of God beyond this parental image (the same goes for Mother), while still somehow keeping the warmth this kind of imagery connotes. It is not easy, but it is worth the effort!

61: Here I would most certainly insert "God" for "he," as explained above.

68: See comments for line 60.

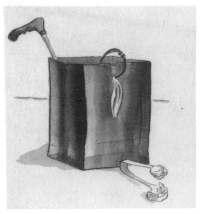

The children's sermon is not meant to be just a nice talk. The message is always pointed—pointed in the direction of the Christian faith. Here the Bible is woven into what is said, by inference and by verse. Not all the Bible, however, is applicable (as already noted). Its primary use is to draw attention to the person of Jesus, to the presence of God, and to how others (those in the Bible) have believed. I emphasize the relevant passages of what Jesus said and did, and especially the passages that speak of the love and goodness of God. At times I mention other biblical themes such as sin, forgiveness, baptism, prayer, and so on. Many of the older children have their own Bibles, and it is my hope that the use of this very important book will cause them to want to read it more often. Thus, the Bible is used—and I try to make this clear to them—because it provides the basis for what we believe.

Recently, a colleague who teaches in the religion department of one of our leading liberal arts colleges commented that almost without exception college students do not know the stories in the Bible. In their church school years they did other things, from reading more contemporary stories (no doubt with good moral content) to cutting and pasting, coloring and drawing. But the biblical stories were not given much emphasis. As a result, for these students, and one suspects this would be true on other campuses, there now is a real void in their thoughts and lives. What an opportunity we have in our respective churches, even in this brief time with the children, to give them this essential grounding in the Bible! Our biblical stories can be most effectively adapted for children's sermons!

An example[39]:

Happy or Sad

Jesus told this story, and I think he'd like me to retell it to you. I'm also sure he won't mind if I use my own words as I tell it.

Once there was a father who had two sons. (If you would like to think of them as a mother and two daughters, that's OK. Again, I don't think Jesus will mind, just as long as we understand what he was trying to say.) The younger came to his father and said, "I want what later will be mine when you are no longer living." The reason he wanted this was because he planned to leave home and live in a country far away. And he needed money to live there. So, his father gave him what he requested, the half that would later be his anyway. And off he went.

Once in that far country, things didn't go according to plan. He soon lost his money in foolish, wasteful, and sinful ways. Having no money and being hungry, he agreed to work for a farmer, who in turn sent him out to feed the pigs. And he didn't even like pigs! He was so hungry, he ate what the pigs ate. Yuk!

Then he remembered his father and his mother and how life was much better at home. He decided to go home, tell his father that he had done wrong, that he no longer deserved to be called his son. His request would be just to work for his father like the hired servants. After all, they were treated better than he was among the pigs.

As he was coming down the road toward his home, his father saw him and ran to greet him, telling him how much he loved him. Then the father said, "Let's have a party, for my son was gone and now is back."

Jesus didn't tell in his story about the happy face

this son must have had. But the son's smile shows through in what Jesus told.

Here's a bit of my artwork showing what I think that big smile must have looked like. . . . Looking at it makes me smile.

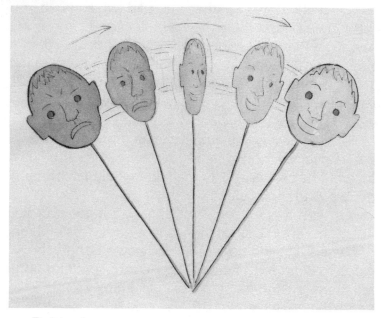

But in the story, not everyone was happy or smiling. The other son, the one who stayed at home and worked hard for his father, didn't like what his younger brother had done. He complained to his father, saying, "Look what your son has done, he wasted the money you gave him. Now he's back, and you're giving him a welcome home party. That makes me sad, for you've never given me a party!"

Here's how his face must have looked. . . . Sad! Angry!

What did the father say to him? This: "Your brother is home, and no matter what he has done wrong, I love him too much to forget about him, or not to let him come home. You have been a good son, and what I have will still be yours. But I am glad your brother is home. Let's be happy!"

Are we unhappy when someone is loved after having done what's wrong? Do we wish they'd get punished instead? Ah, God loves them no matter what, and because of that we're to smile with happiness.

You know, no matter what we do wrong, nor how far we go (or feel) away from God—who knows the wrong we do—we can come back to God, for we are still loved! What a happy thought. It makes me smile!

Two faces. Which is ours? We're loved, no matter what we've done. So smile! Others are loved, too, no matter what. Let's smile, and not frown. That's what Jesus did.

Let us pray.
Dear God: We're so happy you love us—all of us. Amen.

Question: How do we react when, during the children's sermon, some children begin to misbehave? On any given Sunday there is such a wide age variance, which can prove problematic. This is due, of course, to the fact that not all children's attention spans, or interests, are the same. As a result a couple of children may start talking to each other, completely oblivious to what is being said, and disturbing the other children as they try to listen. Or, as happened one Sunday, a vase of flowers had been placed too near and it proved too tempting—one child almost tipped it over onto another's head (needless to say, the flowers were never placed there again!). I vividly remember the time when one little boy pushed another little boy, and then push came to shove. I solved this problem by asking one of the boys to sit next to me, saying, "I need your help. Would you show the other children what is in my brown bag?" It worked! Usually, such a child is too young or immature or is disruptive for a variety of reasons.

Oh, with that private conversation between those two mentioned above, I also looked straight at them and asked in a soft voice, "What do you think?" As I mentioned earlier, one of the cardinal rules I always follow is NO PUT-DOWNS! Yes, from time to time kids will be kids, and it is important to handle the situation with respect. If the children in question are belittled, I feel it is a "negative," which defeats the purpose of this special time and opportunity.

An example:

No Put-downs!

What if I were to say to you:

> "Dummy!"
> "I don't like you."
> "You dress funny."
> "If only you were better looking."
> "You do messy work."
> "I can run faster than you can."
> "You're no good."

"I'm smarter."
"Hey, Fatty." Or, "Beanstalk."
"You lazy so-and-so."
"Who could ever believe you?"
"You're impossible!"

How would that make you feel? Not so good, right? I don't blame you!

Before I go any farther, let me assure each of you that all these things I've just said I don't mean. No, I don't think you are dummies, or that you're not very good-looking, or that you're no good. I think the opposite of you. I like each of you very much.

But, even though you know I didn't mean what I just said to you, hearing it made you feel terrible on the inside. Now didn't it? You don't like being put down, do you? *I* sure don't! And yet, almost every day someone says something to us that is a put-down, something that makes us feel bad about ourselves inside. We may know for a fact that it isn't true, but still it hurts.

How do you think others feel when they hear put-downs from us? . . . You're right, they feel awful!

83

Do you ever give put-downs? A put-down doesn't have to be said in so many words, for it could be just a look. A look? Yes, with a turned-up nose, a turned-down mouth, or with raised eyebrows, like this . . . , saying to that other person, "Who do you think you are anyway?" A motion! Yes, like putting your first finger to the side of your head and twirling it around, like this . . . , thereby saying without a word spoken, "That person is crazy!" Think how that must make that person feel!

You know, every person has something good to be said for herself or himself. Sure, no one is perfect, meaning no one, including ourselves, is without some fault. But what about the good in each of us? If we help that other person feel good about herself or himself, that same person may even be encouraged to be more loving toward others. Let us do as it says in the Bible, "Let us consider how to stir up one another to love and good works, . . . encouraging one another [Heb. 10:24–25b]." Call it a "put-up."

So, let's make a rule and live by it. I've printed it on a big sign. It reads: "NO PUT-DOWNS."

And I have written this rule on a small piece of paper for each of you. Talk it over with your church school teacher and with your parents, if you want to hear more about how best to do this. But start today making this your rule of love.

Let us pray.
Dear God: We're sorry for the put-downs we've said to others, and we'll try our best not to do it again. Amen.

What do you do when you lose it? And I mean *lose it!*
Recently, a child took the sermon away from me. I began
asking a question about birthdays. A hand went up, for
this little fellow's birthday had just passed, and he needed
to talk about it. I listened. When he finished, I resumed
only to have his little hand pop up again. So, I listened
again. When at last he finished, I started on with the
sermon and once more he wanted to say something. Not
wanting to give a put-down, I listened further. By this
time the congregation was beginning to laugh. This wor-
ried me, for if he interpreted their laughter the wrong way,
it could hurt. Rather, he realized he had an audience!
Each time I tried to say something, he butted in, all to
more laughter. The next thing I knew he was next to me,
doing a song and dance. More laughter! (His mother was
in the front pew—with her hands over her face—embarrassed.) I had lost it! No way could I bring the sermon to a
fitting conclusion. I tried to continue a bit, but in hindsight
I should have said, "Let's talk again next Sunday. Amen."
So, a word to the wise: Don't fight it! On those occasions
when you lose it, say "Amen." There will be another time
to try again.

Many themes we use in our children's sermons will

be repeated any number of times throughout the year. That is OK! Can we ever say it all in just one sermon? Of course not! However, when we are reworking a given theme or idea, we need to do so with as much creativity and imagination as we can muster. Focusing once more on the put-up theme, how do we help the children see themselves doing this? With specific examples!

An example:

A Spark Plug

All of us can do some things well, and some things not so well. And I would rather not talk about what I don't do well.

But, this morning I want to mention just one thing at which I'm not good. Please don't tell everyone about this. When it comes to motors, I'm not too good at fixing what goes wrong. Yes, I know a few things about motors, like how they are supposed to work after the key is turned on. But if it doesn't work, when I lift the hood of the car, I just shake my head. It all looks so confusing!

My first thought is where to find an auto mechanic (that's someone who really knows how to fix cars). I look at all those wires and hoses, and I don't know where to begin. Sure, I could learn how to fix my car by reading books on this subject. Or, better yet, I could work with someone who knows a lot about cars and who would be willing to teach me. However, I really

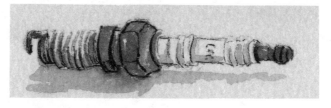

don't have the time to do that. So, when it doesn't work right, or drive as it's supposed to, I take it to the car repair shop.

Here's a part of a car. It's called a "spark plug."

What a spark plug does inside the engine is cause a spark. This explodes the gas, which pushes some parts (called pistons) up and down. These cause some small wheels inside the engine to turn, which moves the parts that go to the big wheels. This is what makes a car move. Now you understand about as much as I do about car engines.

Back to the spark plug. I still don't quite understand how it works. It has no moving parts. Oh, it gets its spark, which is like a little bit of fire that looks like lightning, by being hooked up to the battery. However, as I've been told, the spark plug isn't hooked up, or wired up, directly to the battery. There's something about a thing called an "alternator," and I'm not sure what that is. Anyway, the spark plug gets the car going. Without it, it wouldn't go.

But this I do know. We often speak of a person as being "a spark plug." No, not as in a car. When people are called this, what is really being said about them is that they get things going.

What about you? You do this when you're excited about a new game, and others get excited and want to play it too. Or, when you read a good book and tell about it, this also causes your friends to want to read it. Or, again, when you have a wonderful idea on how to help someone and this makes others get excited about doing the same.

Are you a spark plug?

Jesus was once teaching some people on the side of a mountain and he said, "Let your light so shine . . . that [others] may see your good works, and give glory to

87

your [God] who is in heaven [Matt. 5:16]." That's the spark plug idea! Get the idea?

This week be a spark plug. No, not like the one I have in my hand. What a funny thought! Rather, be one who starts something good happening.

Let us pray.
Dear God: Help us to start something good. Amen.

Earlier I noted that there is a wide age variance in the children who come forward for these sermons. From time to time, I am asked how old a child should be to start coming, and my reply is "When a child wants to come, then it's time, and not before." In like manner, how old is too old? The children will also decide that!

My children's sermons are for children, and *only* for children! Granted, adults also enjoy them. *Gerty's Papa's Civil War,* mentioned in the Preface, has this interesting anecdote:

Other ministers talked just to the adults in the Sunday services and sometimes bored the children. But Gerty's father sometimes talked just to the children.

When he did that, more people came to church than on other days. He talked in a way the children could understand, and they liked to listen to him. Even the adults liked to listen. One Sunday a woman asked for a copy of his talk because she liked it so much. He thought she meant his sermon to the adults. But no, she didn't want that—she wanted a copy of his talk to the children![40]

And in our day, Reuel Howe, in his book *Partners in Preaching, Clergy and Laity in Dialogue,* notes what I have heard expressed:

> Adults frequently say the sermons they really like are those prepared and delivered to children because they are simple, vivid, employ ordinary language, and are concerned about life. They find themselves thinking about these sermons for weeks afterward, whereas some Sunday evening they cannot even remember the sermon that was prepared for and delivered to them in the morning.[41]

Alas! The latter part of Howe's comment gives me heartburn about what is or is not happening for the adults during their sermon time (which goes beyond the scope of this book). It causes me to want to work all the harder on my other sermons. But—back to the children's sermons—I deem it wrong to use this time to speak indirectly to the adults. Yes, they can continue to enjoy listening in; and they may well get more out of it than they do from the adult sermon. However, the children deserve my full attention during their time.

Because it is for the children, I purposefully sit down on their level. To stand, while they sit on the chancel floor, is too much of a power position. It suggests, in essence, that I am really going to tell it *to them—and they had better listen!* Rather, to sit on their eye level is to say that it is a time of sharing. I tell them how important they are.

An example:

Let the Children Come

Just moments ago, you heard me say, "Let the children come." And you came. Here we are, sitting together. Oh, how I look forward to this time. For me, this is one of the most important times in the whole week. I hope you look forward to this time as much as I do. From the way you hurry down the aisles of the church, I think I'm safe in saying that you enjoy coming.

When I see you coming down these aisles each

Sunday, I can't help but think of Jesus and the children. He loved children! Oh, he loved everyone, but he especially loved children. And when he talked with the adults, he also welcomed their children. He invited them right up front where he was seated. How do I know this? Well, it tells about this in the Bible.

One day (and there must have been many days like this) Jesus was teaching people about God, and those who heard him wanted him to give some special attention to their children. But the disciples (twelve close friends who stayed with Jesus every day) thought the children were in the way. They decided among themselves that the children were taking up too much of Jesus' valuable time. We don't know how many children were there that day, but there must have been quite a few. If only we had been there! Of course, all this happened a long time ago, long before you and I were born.

I have in my brown bag a picture of Jesus with the children, or at least two of them. No, not a photo. This was long before cameras were invented. Rather, this is a drawing created by an artist.[42] Take a look. . . .

It says in the Bible that "the disciples rebuked the people [Matt. 19:13]." That means they were telling the parents that they were wrong in bringing their children, and that they should take them away from there so Jesus could continue his teaching.

And what did Jesus do and say about all this? The Bible says that he became "indignant," or upset, with his disciples. He wanted the children there! And he said, "Let the children come, do not hinder them; for to such belongs the kingdom of God [Mark 10:14]." That means that Jesus wanted them present because they were loved by God.

91

I think that is one of the best parts of the whole Bible. What Jesus was saying and doing was meant for you too. In other words, he was saying that children, you and all children, are loved by him and by God. You are important!

Did you know that you are important to Jesus and to God? And that you are loved by them? That is what Jesus came to tell you, and all of us. This is the most important truth of all! God is love, and that means God loves you and me and all of us.

Let us pray.
Dear God: Thank you for loving us. Amen.

Each children's sermon is concluded with a one-sentence prayer. The prayer's purpose is threefold. (1) It provides a fitting ending. I have heard children's sermons just end, and then heard myself say, "Oh, it's over?" I feel a prayer is really the most appropriate way to conclude. In fact, the children I am with each Sunday have come to expect me to conclude with a prayer. If I failed to pray before they left, which I never have, I can just imagine some child saying, "Aren't we going to pray?" (2) The prayer's intent is to encapsulate the essence of the sermon with either a note of thanks or a request for help in doing what we have discussed together, or to express a desire to do what is right and good. I make no apology for emphasizing the main point of the sermon in the prayer, which is not another attempt to preach the sermon's essence. Rather, I hope the children will lift up this point in their prayerful thoughts to God. (3) Not only is this a fitting conclusion of the children's sermon, but it also reminds the children to pray. My eyes are closed, which prevents me from seeing how intent they really are at this moment, though I am told that the children do fold their hands and bow their heads. I hope they feel as I do, that we are at this moment talking with God, even though it be ever so brief. And I pray that as we have prayed together, they in turn will also pray. All we do, as well as say, has an impact on even the youngest among us.

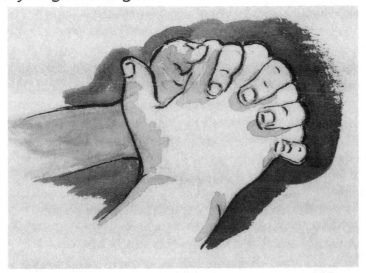

P.S. (Prayer Suggestion): I always begin each prayer with "Dear God." Not only is it a warm, loving way to address God, it also solves the problem of continually having to find a new way to begin to pray. Many prayers address God in styles both too adult and not inclusive. In short, this is the way it works best for me, and I offer it as a suggestion for you to consider.

In fact, this book is just that, suggestions you might consider, ones that have worked for me in my children's sermons. It is my hope that these suggestions will help in your work with children.

It is an intriguing title John Westerhoff uses for his book *Will Our Children Have Faith?* More than intriguing, it is haunting and scary in a world which seems less *in* church. Granted, in the last few years we have seen a resurgence of growth in the more conservative churches. Some have said that this will bring a new spirit in all the churches, and the church will yet see a new day. Yes, there does seem to be growing interest in the more moderate to liberal churches in talking about what it is we really do believe, and in living that faith in today's world. In part, I do believe the conservative ripple-effect has washed our own moderate to liberal shores, but even more I feel our own people pine for more meaning and purpose in their lives. There is the working of God's Spirit in our midst! Augustine's words keep coming back to us, "Thou has made us for thyself, and our hearts are restless until they find rest in thee."[43]

However, having recognized this renewal going on in our midst and in our lives, there is much in the church (generally speaking) that is questionable. Some expressions of the faith are nothing but pie-in-the-sky religion ("Don't worry, for in the sweet by-and-by . . ."). Others have a more self-centered than Christ-centered emphasis ("Lord, if you will do this for me, I'll . . ."). Frequently, it is rather one-issue oriented ("The Golden Rule is all I need"). It is too narrowly expressed too much of the time ("If you don't believe or do as I do, then your Christianity is suspect"). At times, it is a damning religious message ("If you don't do thus and so, God will get you!"). And, then, there are those who are only religious spectators in the pew ("Don't ask me to do anything, for I'm too involved at the office, or at . . ."). When all this is taken into account, and given a proper perspective, it makes many of us wonder what effect all this popular religion will have on our children. Will they have faith, the kind that is true, good, healthy, viable, dynamic, persistent, creative, and loyal? The future of our children, the church's children, and all God's children needs to be uppermost in our thoughts. I am especially concerned about this faith issue. It does matter what our children believe, for what they believe will affect how they live, and how they live will make a difference for the future of the church and the world.

So, we in the church have the awesome and special task of seeing to it that our children's religious grounding is solid. Its curriculum and classroom work is important and indispensable. Also, a good youth group experience when that time comes, is helpful, provided it has good guidance in integrating the faith into the rationale of loving and caring relationships. Not to be overlooked is the children's sermon, for it too needs to be viewed as being woven into the whole church's tapestry of Christian education. It is a complement to the other educational activities done toward this end, and not something set apart to itself. This underscores that we all need to work together in making the faith we preach and teach and live a more integral part of our ministry to our children.

And why? Ours is the divine commission to teach the faith to our children by precept and example. Surely this is what Jesus had in mind when he said, "Let the children come unto me, do not hinder them; for to such belongs the kingdom of God [Mark 10:14]."

95

It is in this context that children's sermons find their proper niche in the church. And the learning takes place in the act of worship! Those who object, claiming that the time spent is an intrusion on the worship's solemnity, fail to realize the impact on our children.

The question is ever before us, "Will our children have faith?" Yes, if we will do our part in the teaching and

in the encouragement of the Faith. But first we need to be more responsive to the many "Whys?" our children have, and then to learn better how to do the "how-to's" of this kind of sermon.

My best to you, and to your children.

Notes

1. Lewis Carroll, *Alice's Adventures in Wonderland,* ch. 1, first paragraph.

2. Church newsletter. Mr. Cross was the pastor of the First Congregational Church, Colorado Springs, Colorado, from 1876 to 1881.

3. *The Brown Bag* (1978), *Another Brown Bag* (1980), and *One More Brown Bag* (1983), a trilogy of children's sermon books published by The Pilgrim Press, New York.

4. The Rev. Dr. Robert Frykholm is the senior pastor of the First Baptist Church, Colorado Springs, Colorado.

5. Sara Lynn Weatherman is the Christian education director of the First Congregational Church, United Church of Christ, Colorado Springs, Colorado.

6. The Rev. Dr. Annabel Clark lives in Littleton, Colorado, has a Ph.D. in theater and an M.Div. degree from The Iliff School of Theology, Denver, Colorado.

7. Dr. P. Roy Brammell is a retired educator who chaired the School of Education at the University of Connecticut for many years and then taught at Southern Illinois University. A former parishioner of the author, he now lives in Boulder, Colorado.

8. Lavonne Eliason, a homemaker and former parishioner, lives in Cañon City, Colorado.

9. Mary Lou Anderson is the illustrator of my previous three books and a member of First Congregational Church, UCC, Colorado Springs, Colorado.

10. Gayle, a wonderful spouse, is a valuable helper in my "doing" of children's sermons (many of the ideas incorporated into this book she first shared with me). I benefit from her many years as an elementary teacher and her innate good sense about how to communicate with children.

11. Roger L. Shinn, *The Educational Mission of Our Church* (Boston/Philadelphia: United Church Press, 1962),

pp. 39–40. I have taken the liberty of making this quote inclusive, to which I am sure Dr. Shinn would agree.

12. John Macquarrie, *Principles of Christian Theology* (New York: Charles Scribner's Sons, 1966), p. 6. Copyright © 1966, 1977 John Macquarrie. Reprinted with the permission of Charles Scribner's Sons.

13. John H. Westerhoff III, *Values for Tomorrow's Children* (New York: The Pilgrim Press, 1970, 1979), pp. 9–10.

14. Copyright © 1986 Brian Wren. Used with permission.

15. Jean Piaget completed twenty-eight books while writing ten more in collaboration with two colleagues, Alina Szeminska and Bärbel Inhelder. The ones I recommend pertain to specific areas of interest that impact our understanding of children as we prepare our children's sermons: Perception: *The Mechanisms of Perception* (New York: Basic Books, 1969); Reality: *The Construction of Reality in the Child* (New York: Basic Books, 1954); Memory: with Inhelder, *Mental Imagery in the Child* (New York: Basic Books, 1971); Imitation: *Play, Dreams, and Imitation in Childhood* (New York: W.W. Norton & Co., 1962); Language: *The Language and Thought of the Child* (New York: Harcourt, Brace, 1926); Time: *The Child's Conception of Time* (London: Routledge & Kegan Paul, 1969); Morality: *The Moral Judgment of the Child* (New York: Free Press, 1965); also *Six Psychological Studies* (New York: Random House, 1967); plus Mary Ann Spencer Palaski, *Understanding Piaget* (New York: Harper & Row, 1980). I have also greatly benefited from *Children and Adolescents: Interpretive Essays on Jean Piaget,* by David Elkin (New York: Oxford University Press, 1970). Piaget died September 16, 1980, the giant in the field of developmental psychology (or child development).

16. Lawrence Kohlberg, Harvard psychologist, has built on the works of Piaget. His writings are well worth reading, in particular his "Moral Stages and Moralization," in *Moral Development and Behavior,* ed. Lickona (New York: Holt, Rinehart and Winston, 1976). Also, you may want to read his "The Claim of Moral Adequacy of a Highest Stage of Moral

Judgment," *The Journal of Philosophy* 70 (Oct. 25, 1973):642, and "The Child as Moral Philosopher," in *Moral Education,* ed. Barry I. Chasan and Jonas F. Soltis (New York: Teachers College Press, 1974).

17. James Fowler's "Life/Faith Patterns" in Jim Fowler and Sam Keen, *Life Maps: Conversations on the Journey of Faith,* ed. Jerome Berryman (Waco, TX: Word Books, 1978). Also, read "Stages in Faith: The Structural-Developmental Approach," in *Values and Moral Development,* ed. Thomas C. Hennessy (Paramus, NJ: Paulist/Newman Press, 1976).

18. Erik Erikson's "Growth and Crises of the Healthy Personality," *Identity and the Life Cycle: Selected Papers (Psychological Issues),* vol. 1, no. 1 (New York: International Press, 1959). Also, *Childhood and Society* (New York: W.W. Norton & Co., 1950, 1963).

19. Mary M. Wilcox, *Developmental Journey* (Nashville: Abingdon Press, 1979). This is an excellent book.

20. Fred B. Craddock, *Overhearing the Gospel* (Nashville: Parthenon Press, 1978), pp. 10–11. Used with permission.

21. *Webster's Ninth New Collegiate Edition* (Springfield, MA: Merriam-Webster, Inc., 1986), p. 1172. Used with permission.

22. Elizabeth Griffen, *A Dog's Book of Bugs* (New York: Atheneum, 1967). Drawing of book cover used with permission of the artist, Peter Parnall.

23. Ibid. Copyright © 1967 Elizabeth Griffen. Reprinted with the permission of Atheneum Publishers.

24. Ibid.

25. Kornei Chukovsky, *From Two to Five,* ed. and trans. Miriam Morton (Berkeley: University of California Press, 1963), p. 21. Used with permission.

26. *Henry V,* III, ii, 40.

27. Watty Piper, *The Little Engine That Could* (New York: Platt & Munk, 1961). Used with permission of Grosset & Dunlap.

28. *The Ministers Manual,* ed. Charles L. Wallis (1974 ed.; New York: Harper & Row), p. 257. Copyright © 1973 by

Charles L. Wallis. All rights reserved. Used by permission.

29. *The Brown Bag* (New York: The Pilgrim Press, 1978), p. 11.

30. Iris V. Cully, *Christian Child Development* (San Francisco: Harper & Row, 1979), pp. 118–19. Used with permission.

31. Correspondence dated March 10, 1981.

32. Dr. Sockman taught homiletics at Union Theological Seminary, New York, and for forty-four years, 1917 to 1961, served as minister of Christ Church (Methodist), New York.

33. From *The Elements of Style,* Third Edition, by William Strunk Jr. and E.B. White, p. 72. Copyright © 1979 by Macmillan Publishing Company. Reproduced by permission of the publisher.

34. Ibid.

35. John H. Westerhoff III, *Will Our Children Have Faith?* (New York: Seabury Press, 1976), p. 33. Used with permission of Harper & Row.

36. *Inclusive Language Guidelines for Use and Study in the United Church of Christ,* June 1980, United Church of Christ, Church Leadership Resources, St. Louis, p. 1.

37. Dr. Brueggemann made this observation in a D.Min. class at Eden Theological Seminary, Webster Groves, Missouri, during the summer of 1981, in a course on the Psalms.

38. *Inclusive Language Guidelines,* p. 1.

39. This sermon is based on the parable of the prodigal son, Luke 15:11–32.

40. William H. Armstrong in Preface to Edward Parmelee Smith, *Gerty's Papa's Civil War* (New York: The Pilgrim Press, 1984), p. xiii.

41. Reuel Howe, *Partners in Preaching, Clergy and Laity in Dialogue* (New York: Seabury Press, 1967), p. 27. Used with permission of Harper & Row.

42. The drawing on page 90, by Mary Lou Anderson, is of "The Children's Friend" by Roger H. Martin, © 1963, United Church Press. The original picture was used for the sermon.

43. Augustine, *The Confessions,* Book I, 1.